The Hidden Bible

Unearthing the Bible's Artistic Secrets

Essays on Biblical Literature

A selection of other books by Yair Mazor:

Hounding the Hound of the Baskervilles
A Poetic Portrait of the Detective Novel

Poetic Acrobat:
The Poetry of Ronny Someck

Nocturnal Lament:
The Poetry of David Fogel and Modern Hebrew Poetry

Broken Twig:
The Poetry of Dalia Ravikovich and Modern Hebrew Poetry

Bridled Bird:
The Poetry of Nathan Zach and Modern Hebrew Poetry

The Flower and the Fury:
The Poetry of Yonah Wollach and Modern Hebrew Poetry

Who Wrought the Bible? Unveiling the Bible's Aesthetic Secrets

Israeli Poetry of the Holocaust

Somber Lust: The Art of Amos Oz"

Pain, Pining, and Pine Trees: Contemporary Hebrew Poetry

The Triple Cord: Agnon, Hamsun, Strindberg:
Where Hebrew and Scandinavian Meet

The Poetry of Asher Reich: Portrait of a Hebrew Poet

The Hidden Bible

Unearthing the Bible's
Artistic Secrets

Essays on Biblical Literature

YAIR MAZOR

HenschelHAUS Publishing, Inc.
Milwaukee, Wisconsin

Published by
HenschelHAUS Publishing, Inc.
www.henschelHAUSbooks.com

ISBN: 978159598-039-7
E-ISBN:978159598-194-3
LCCN: 2017948442

For Bilha,

"I accounted to your favor
The devotion of your youth
Your love as a bride—
How you followed me in the wilderness
In a land not sown."

(Jeremiah 2: 2,3)

"This world is full of obvious things which nobody by any chance even observes."
—Sherlock Holmes in *The Hound of the Baskervilles*

"You have heard about me, Mr. Holmes," she cried, "else how could you know all that?"

"Never mind," said Holmes laughingly. "It is my business to know things. Perhaps I have trained myself to see what others overlook."
—Sherlock Holmes in *A Case of Identity*

H. CASTELLI

TABLE OF CONTENTS

PREFACE

This book addresses and probes selected texts and books of the Hebrew Bible while focusing on the literariness of the Bible (the Hebrew Bible). Indeed, major parts of the Bible are not "pure" literature (*belles lettres*) *per se,* as their most prominent goal is not aesthetic/artistic (although their literariness is praiseworthy), rather molding and serving, delivering a pragmatic message. Such a message can be liturgical, national, political, historical, educational, moral, social, and more. For instance, biblical prophesies convey many messages, among them liturgical, legal, moral, historical, national, political and social.

Hence, despite the singular, laudable literary nature of prophesies (as well as books such as Chronicles (I, II), Proverbs, Samuel (I, II) Kings (I, II), Judges, even Psalms, and others), they cannot be considered literature *per se*, as their major goal is not literary, but rather pragmatic (that observation is discussed and justified in the following introduction). Thus, this book of aesthetic and biblical scholarship does not only probe and analyze the singular literary/aesthetic qualities of many biblical texts, as it simultaneously investigates the artistic devices, patterns, and mechanisms that are sculpted and "installed" in those biblical texts to convey and enhance their messages.

This book addresses a target audience which is not limited to biblical and literary scholars. It addresses diverse professional and non-professional readers who possess interest in both the Hebrew Bible and literature in general. In this light, the book adopts the following scholarly policy, one which is as easily accessible as possible and is considerably user-friendly. The writing policy consists of the following three practices:

1) The language of the book is devoid of professional jargon;

2) Most of the chapters in this book are short, some very short;

3) I have refrained from using footnotes, with one exception, as they tend to disrupt the flow of the text.

In addition, please note that there is more than one policy of transliterating biblical Hebrew into the English language. I must confess, however, that I find those policies (or at least some parts of them) too "opaque," as they introduce stumbling blocks on the desirably fluent flow of accurately pronouncing the transliterated biblical Hebrew syllables and words .

Hebrew is my native tongue, I have read the Bible for more than sixty years now, and I have professionally investigated the Bible for more than thirty-five years. Nevertheless, I still find those methods of transliteration regretfully unfriendly for the user. For that reason, the policy of transliteration practiced and displayed in this book is phonetically oriented, one that ensures that the reader (notably the unprofessional reader) will not encounter any difficulty in accurately pronouncing the transliterated biblical Hebrew syllables and words.

INTRODUCTION

As stated in the Preface, this book does not only analyze the spectacular literariness of numerous texts of the Hebrew Bible, it also studies and portrays the ramified aesthetic means that are shaped and cultivated by those biblical texts and convey "practical" messages. Indeed, this book is a book of science, a book of the science of literature, a book of the science of the art of biblical literature. Arguments like the latter may seem at first glance at least to be quite questionable, while demanding cogent explanations and clarifications. Thus, these arguments and statements yield the following questions:

- What is the definition of literature?
- What is the definition of art?
- What is the definition of science?
- Is literature, including biblical literature, science?
- Can literature be science?

To be able to respond persuasively to these questions, one must articulate the following two questions:

- What is the definition of a definition?
- What makes a definition valid?

All these questions have to provide plausible answers prior to launching the scientific, artistic/aesthetic, literary approach to the Bible.

What is science? It seems as an elementary question, that easily meets an elementary answer. As Sherlock Holmes said to his companion, Dr. Watson: "Elementary, Watson, elementary." However, are our questions so elementary?

Hence, when you ask an educated person what is science he/she would probably say, "science is biology, zoology, chemistry, physics, mathematics, microbiology, and other fields of study of similar nature. However, what is that nature? And why is not the study of literature, of history, of philosophy, of art, not science?

It seems that the answer, "science is biology," etc. confuses between the following two: the nature of the investigation of a certain field of study, and the nature of that field of study itself. Hence, science is not a certain field of study. Biology is not science, chemistry is not science, physics is not science, mathematics is not science, and so on.

The response to the latter statements is the following. Science is not a certain field of study, a certain bulk of knowledge. Science is the *way* in which that specific field of study is investigated. What is that way of investigation? The scientist develops a theory, and then he/she develops a methodology that derives from that theory. Following the latter, the scientist practices that methodology while trying to find out whether his/her theory is valid or if it is wrong.

If the theory is valid, the scientist may resume his/her investigation by making the theory more detailed, more intricate, more comprehensive, more accurate, more sophisticated. However, if the application of the methodology to the theory proves that the theory is invalid, the scientist is compelled to go back to the drawing board, to reformulate his or her theory, and launch again the systematic procedure of putting to test the updated (or new) theory, while systematically utilizing the methodology.

Thus, science is not a certain field of study, science is the systematic, methodological *way* in which the specific field of study is investigated. Accordingly, while biology is not science, studying systematically biology, while applying to that study theory and methodology, is science. That is the science of biology.

That is also the study of literature or other fields of the humanities, such as history, philosophy, as well as other fields of study, such as sociology and psychology.

In other words, literature is not science, but rather, a systematic study of literature (theory, methodology) is science. Science is not the field of knowledge, but the *way* in which the field of knowledge is studied. Thus the Bible is not science, but the systematic way in which the Bible is investigated (theory, methodology) is science.

Indeed, both theory and methodology of the sciences of the humanities (literature, for instance) are very far from the sophistication and precision of the theory and methodology of biology, physics, chemistry, mathematics, and so on. Yet arguing that the study of literature is not science, since its theory and methodology lag far behind the theory and methodology of biology, for instance, is like arguing that a certain chair is not a chair since it aggravates my lower back, or because one of its legs is broken.

We must therefore be very careful not to confuse an objective definition with subjective judgment/evaluation.

The fashion in which we determine that a certain field of study is science, we practically provide with a definition of that field of study.

Now we know the definition of science. It is time to articulate the definition of a definition. A definition has to be broad enough to include as many items as possible, and specific enough to avoid an "invasion" to the definition of items that do not belong to that definition. For instance, if one defines a table as a piece of furniture, the definition is valid but too broad, too "elastic." Hence, such a definition can include a chair, a book shelf, a sofa, a night stand, a dresser, and so on. However, once we define a table as a piece of furniture on which we eat or write, the definition is very valid indeed: it includes all the tables in the world and it prevents non-relevant items to "invade" that definition.

And what about art? How can one define art? And how can one define the art of literature? In order to answer cogently those two questions, one can use the following example. A person enters a museum. He is told that the art museum purchased the most exquisite work of art, the most singular painting, for $2 million. That person cultivates the most elevated expectations. After all, art is his passion and he is more than eager to see that remarkably praiseworthy work of art, the newly purchased painting, the $2 million price tag comes from the pockets of the taxpayers.

Introduction

He is standing in a very long line of people who share his ardent eagerness to view that "sublime" painting. Also, the day is very hot and equally humid. Nevertheless, he is willing to sacrifice his comfort for the sake of viewing such a marvelous painting. Eventually, he reaches the painting. The aesthetically spellbinding painting looks like this:

The man almost collapses, almost passes out. After he regains his ability to speak, however, he starts screaming and ranting, "This is a disgrace! This is a hoax! This is not a painting! This is a shame! This is not a work of art! This is idle chatter probably done by a child! This is nonsense! This is garbage! This is not art!"

Emotionally bruised and physically exhausted, the man heads to the cafeteria to calm himself down with a cup of coffee. He pays for the coffee and takes it to a small table. However, his "dose" of disheartening experiences is not over yet. The coffee is cold and tasteless, and suddenly, the chair he is sitting on breaks and he finds himself lying on the floor.

Once again, the man starts yelling. He started screaming again: "What kind of worthless coffee do you serve here? How dare you keep such shamefully ramshackle, rickety chairs?"

Having fallen to the floor not once, but twice, he is excruciatingly frustrated and upset. His throat hurts from screaming two times. However, there is a significant difference between his two upsetting experiences.

In the case of the painting, he screamed that it is not a work of art. In the case of the cold, tasteless coffee and the flimsy chair, he did not scream that it was *not* coffee and it was *not* a chair. In other words, the harried patron contested the definition of the painting as a work of art, while in the case of the coffee and the chair, he did not contest their definitions as coffee and a chair.

What could be the reason for such a distinction between artwork on the one hand, and coffee and table on the other? The reason is probably associated with the Romantic period (19th century) of art. Indeed, in ancient days, the days of Aristotle and Plato (5th and 4th centuries BCE), an artist was considered a craftsman.

Plato even fervently argued that the artist should be evicted from society as he endorsed moral corruption by painting nature instead of painting the sublime idea of nature. According to Plato's theory, each and every object in the world is an imitation of its singularly enticing and perfect idea. Thus if the painter, for instance, paints a tree, and does not aspire to imitate the idea of a tree, he deliberately imitates an imitation, and not the original. In this way, he practices and advocates moral corruption.

Also in the Middle Ages, the artist was also considered a craftsman who had a guild of his own like other craftsmen, such as bakers, carpenters, chimney cleaners, shoemakers, blacksmiths, tailors, and others.

The latter perspective, however, changed dramatically during the Romantic period (end of the 18th century and the beginning of the 19th century) in art in Western Europe. During that period, the artist was placed on the most elevated pedestal: his creativity and artfulness had been considered of the most lofty, praiseworthy nature. Hence, since the artist was "worshiped" so passionately, also his works of art were ardently admired and were considered to be of the most singular, spellbinding value. Correspondingly, people were driven to the wrong assumption that the objective definition of art equals the subjective appreciation of art.

That is exactly what happened in the museum to the unlucky art lover. He had been "fed" by the wrong belief that art, by its very nature, must possess a remarkably worthy value. "Praiseworthy value" is indeed a subjective evaluation, one that does not belong to the definition of art. Hence, a chair is still a chair even when it is dangerously rickety. Coffee is still coffee even when it is cold and tasteless. And a painting is still a work of art, even when everybody determines that it is a very poor quality painting.

Since we relate to the nature of art, and since we will later address the definition of literature as a work of art and the definition of some biblical books as works of art *per se*, we must first define "art."

Hereby, I suggest the following definition of art. A work of art is an object that was either created by a person, or molded by a person, or rearranged by a person (such as moving the object from here to there), and that was created/molded/rearranged by a person (NOT by nature) for an aesthetic purpose ONLY, and NOT for a practical purpose.

Indeed, all artistic objects (paintings, sculptures, music, dance, drama, literature, etc.) are "covered" by that definition. A sculpture is art since it is an object that was created by a person while making its aesthetic purpose its sole purpose of that creation. The aesthetic purpose is the one that aims to "communicate" with the art target audience on the grounds of emotion, tradition, education, psychology, and mental faculties.

Consider, for instance, the following examples. A sculptor finds a large rock in a field. He appreciates it and carries it to the museum, where it is displayed. The sculptor created a work of art since he rearranged (moved it from the field to the museum) the rock and exhibited it in the museum for an aesthetic purpose, one that triggers and ignites an aesthetic response by the target audience.

Even if all onlookers blatantly disdain that newly created work of art, it is still a work of art since it meets the definition of a work of art. Perhaps it is a poor work of art, but the latter is a subjective evaluation/judgment that cannot be included in the realm of the objective definition.

The French artist Marcel Duchamp exhibited a urinal in the museum and entitled it "fountain." Marcel Duchamp is an artist. Hence he rearranged the artistic object by taking it from the bathroom to the museum. Indeed, the urinal, prior to the artistic act of the artist, was a practical object that had been created for one specific, practical human purpose. It was not art. However, once the urinal was moved from the bathroom to the museum, its practical, non-artistic purpose was suspended and the aesthetic purpose took over, as meager as it may be. Hence, even poor art is still art, just as a ramshackle chair is still a chair.

The following joke seems to introduce effectively the definition of art. A man is roaming about the huge exhibition halls in the immensely large museum Le Louvre in Paris. Indeed, he admires greatly the countless works of art exhibited in that magnificent museum. However, he is exceedingly exhausted. He is looking for a quiet corner to rest. Suddenly he notices the most incredibly enticing large chair, placed in the corner of the exhibition hall. He sits on that breathtaking, marvelous, artistically appealing chair with a sigh of relief.

However, his relief does not last for even a single minute. One of the museum guards is hurrying toward the man, his face red with fury.

"What are you doing?" the guard rebukes the man in a raised voice. "Don't you realize that this is the throne of the King of France, Louis the 14th, who is known as the Sun King? Get down from this throne immediately!"

The man smiles and says quietly: "No problem. Once the king returns, I will give him back the chair..."

Indeed, when that artistically breathtaking throne was sculpted for the king, it was a practical object despite its overwhelming artistry. The practical purpose of the throne was to provide the king with a seat, a chair. The practical purpose of the throne "clouded" the prominence of its artistic value.

When the throne was exhibited in the museum, however, its practical function was "muted" or suspended, and the artistic function took over. When the exhausted man sat on the chair, he (unconsciously) returned the throne to its initial practical purpose while "muting" the artistic function of the throne, as enchanting as it was. However, when the patron stepped down from the throne, he again suspended its practical purpose. He "resurrected"

Introduction

the "silenced," the suspended artistic function of the throne, and made it again an object of art.

The watch on my wrist is quite pleasant looking. It does possess a modest aesthetic value. However, it is not a work of art since its main function is not artistic, but rather practical—to tell me the time. Nevertheless, once I am permitted to exhibit it on the wall of the museum, I suspend its practical function and give priority to its artistic qualities, as modest as they may be. The watch continues to tell the time, but that practical function has been "eclipsed" by its aesthetic function. Hence my watch can become a work of art and I can become an artist.

Is it so easy to be an artist? Practically, yes. Also a child who is painting in preschool is an artist no less than Rembrandt. Both of them create objects that meet the definition of art. However, now the issue of subjective evaluation is introduced and regretfully, there is no way whatsoever to turn that subjective evaluation into a reliable, objective judgment.

Once I decide that I have had enough with being an artist and remove the watch from the museum wall, placing it once again on my wrist, I "mute" the aesthetic function of the watch and again give priority to its practical purpose and function.

Once the general definition of art is formulated, the definition of the art of literature is on the threshold. Accordingly, a work of literature, of *belles lettres*, is a work of art that was created in the verbal medium. And what about the sub-definitions of poetry, prose, and drama?

Poetry is a work of art in which the length of the line is determined by the poet, for aesthetic reasons, while in

prose, the publisher is the one who determines the length of the line according to practical reasons, mostly the required format of the book (a large one or a small one) that will meet best the preferences of the book market. Drama is a work of literature in which there is no narrator and the text consists of dialogues, monologues, and soliloquies.

That and more. A book of history can be composed in the most admirable, uplifting literary style. Nevertheless, it is *not* literature, since its major purpose and function are entirely practical, while its magnificent literary style comes second, lagging behind its practical purpose and function.

Indeed, this is exactly the issue with biblical literature. Many parts of biblical literature are not literature *per se*, as their first purpose and prime function are practical. The Bible very frequently has had a practical, "earthly" purpose: to mold and deliver a message, such as liturgical, moral, ideological, social, historical, tribal, pedagogical (like the Book of Proverbs), national, legal, educational, comforting or chastising (like many of the books of the prophets, which convey prophecies of either blatant rebuke or soothing comfort.) Hence, while some chapters of this book study "pure" biblical literature, *per se*, other chapters of this book investigate the namified, sophisticated devices, patterns, and mechanisms that are "rooted" in the biblical texts to mold, enhance, and convey their "practical" messages.

How Literary Devices, Patterns, and Mechanisms Rooted in the Biblical Text Serve and Enhance its Message

The following examples seem to plausibly demonstrate how the biblical text "cultivates," utilizes and practices aesthetic mechanisms and literary devices to manifest and deliver its practical message in the most persuasive fashion.

In Genesis 11 and 12, one reads the following:

> Terah took his son Abram, his grandson
> Lot....and they left the city of Ur and launched
> their voyage to the land of Canaan and they
> reached Haran...the days of Terah came to 205
> years and Terah died in Haran.
>
> And God said to Abram, "Leave your country,
> your homeland and your father's house and go
> to the country which I will show you."

These two very short paragraphs seem to introduce numerous question marks. Why did Terah decide to leave his birthplace, his home city, the prosperous, commercial city, cultural city of Ur, and to resettle in the land of Canaan, a poor land of shepherds and nomads? What did he try to gain by such a drastic, indeed dramatic, move? And how did he know about that distant land, hundreds of kilometers away from him? After all, in those ancient days (probably around 1,800 [2,100?] BCE) there were no means of communication, such as telephone or cellular phones, or letters (except among the nobility and royal courts, whose educated counselors could engrave communications on clay), or radio, or television, or telegraph or the Internet.

Hence, how did Terah learn about the land of Canaan, and what did he know about that distant, poor land? And once they were heading for the land of Canaan, why did they stop in Haran, why did they settle, dwell (*vayeshvu*) in Haran while neglecting the land of Canaan?

That and more. Why did God approach Abram? What was so special about Abram that made him the first lofty prophet of God, the one who represented God when dealing with people? What did Abram know about God? Did he have even a sliver of knowledge about God? And when God decided to appear in front of Abram (How? In what way? How many burning, unconsumed bushes can burn...?) why did God say nothing to Abram about his sacred mission—to be the first prophet of God, the one who is expected to herald the holy word of God, the one who will be the forefather of the chosen people?

Why does God speak to Abram like a realtor: I want you to leave this place and sojourn in that place? Why does Abram obey God without raising even one single question, despite the fact that God's command will drastically change his life, from then on until his last day? Why does not Abram ask the most elementary, naturally expected question: Why me?

Most certainly, all those question marks dramatically draw the curious attention of the reader, who is over-whelmed by so many pressing question marks. The eager curiosity of the reader becomes the most excruciating one.

Indeed, here there are two separate stories which the skillful biblical writer weaves together: the story about Terah, Abram's father, and the story about Abram. Both stories ignite the reader's curiosity: why did all those things happen the way they happened?

It seems that the enigma of Terah's story blazed the trail to Abram's story. The only way to explain the enigmas of Terah's story is the following. Terah was probably "mobilized" by God, although he did not realize it. Terah was a tool God utilized to bring Abram to the Holy Land, to the Promised Land.

Terah had to die in Haran, however. That was God's wish to enable Abram to be the very first one who entered the Holy/Promised Land.

And why did God not share with Abram the sacred facts that he is going to be the first prophet of God, the forefather of the chosen people?

God deliberately refrained from telling Abram all of that. Accordingly, the text demonstrates Abram's pious belief in God, of whom he never heard before, and he follows the order of God without asking *Why, why me?* Abram's absolute, praiseworthy belief in God reached the most elevated vertex.

That and more. Does God not know history? Why does He order Abram to leave behind him his country, his homeland, his father's house, while Abram had already done all of that? The answer is the following. God "failed" to recall that Abram already obeyed His command (to leave behind him his country, his homeland, his father's house while heading for the land of Canaan), since whatever happened to Abram prior to God's appearance to him, before he became the first chosen prophet of God, is irrelevant, is devoid of importance. The history of the chosen people begins only after God "anoints" Abram, and whatever happened before that is not important.

This way, the "showers" of questions combine the two stories, while creating a causal connection between Terah's story and Abram's story. Thus Terah is "mobilized" by God to lead Abram to the Promised Land. However, Terah must die before reaching the Promised Land, since Abram, the chosen prophet, is the one who should be the very first one who enters the Promised Land.

Hence, the text being discussed introduces numerous enigmatic questions. All of them lead the reader to learn about the way God chose Abram to be His prophet (although there is no explanation for why Abram was the one who had been chosen by God and why the land of Canaan was chosen by God to be the Promised Land). Thus, despite the fact that there are numerous enigmatic questions, at the end of the day they guide and direct the reader to realize that all of them are associated with one character—Abram.

Each and every enigmatic question is an aesthetic-rhetorical device, since each of them affects and shapes

the reading and comprehension process. This way, the numerous enigmatic questions operate in the capacity of rhetorical vehicles (dense, aesthetic mechanisms) that lead the reader to comprehend the latent, liturgical, historical meaning of the text in focus.

That latent, liturgical, historical meaning is God's choosing Abram to be His first prophet, the one who will be the first one to receive, accept, and embrace the faith in one formless, abstract God, the one who will be the first forefather of the chosen people.

Another aesthetic device that guides, directs, and dictates effectively the reading and comprehension process is the following one. When Moses descends from Mount Sinai, the holy mountain of God, and introduces the Ten Commandments to the Israelites, they respond with following two (in Hebrew) words: *na'asseh ve-nishmah.* "We will "do" (follow, perform, God's commandments) and we shall listen to them (Exodus 24;7).

That and more. When Joshua is about to say his last, final farewell to all earthly things, he stresses again the absolute, doubtless, crucial need to worship God with no hesitance whatsoever. The Israelites respond with the following words: "We shall worship God and we shall listen to Him" (Joshua, 24; 24).

The two cases in which the Israelites' deliver their two responses to God's commandments, are indeed one. Hence the Israelites, upon being introduced to God's commandments, respond with following words: "We shall fulfill ("do") God's commandments and we shall listen to God's commandments."

The order of presentation hereby displayed is most certainly illogical: first they will worship God, will fulfill ("do") God's commandments, and only later will they listen to God's commandments? This order of presentation upsets and contradicts elementary logic. Accordingly, the logical order of presentation is the very opposite from the one the Israelites practice: first, one should listen to God's commandments, and only later, if one finds those commandments suitable, one shall follow and fulfill those commandments.

However, the illogical order of presentation in this textual continuum is a compositional device: the way in which the text is constructed, the way in which the text is composed. In this case, the compositional device conceives and yields a rhetorical device that is based on surprise, the way in which the compositional device effects, directs and dictates the way in which the text's target audience reacts to the compositional device. Since in this case, the compositional device is illogical, the rhetorical device that stems from the compositional device stresses the illogical, enigmatic, surprising nature of the compositional device.

Both aesthetic devices, however, underline the Israelites' pious faith in God: first, they will "do," will follow and fulfill God's commandments (without even listening to them) and only later will they listen to those commandments.

Hence, the aesthetic mechanism practiced and displayed by this text (which consists of two Hebrew words only in the book of Exodus) is constructed and operates like a domino effect: a compositional device causally leads to a rhetorical device (surprise), and the rhetorical device leads to the latent ideological-liturgical message of the text, demonstrating the pure, pious belief in God practiced and displayed by the Israelites. Hence the latter is a very elucidating case that plausibly demonstrates how the biblical aesthetic mechanism effectively serves the text's ideological, liturgical message.

Another example: Chapter 2 in Genesis, verses 18 through 20, reads as follows:

> The Lord God (both sources J [Jehova/Yahweh]
> and E [Elohim] amalgmated said 'It is not good
> for the man/Adam to stay alone; hence I will
> create for him a spouse/mate ("fitting helper",
> ezer kenegdoh). And the Lord God created from
> the earth all the beasts of the field and all the

birds of the sky and He brought them to Adam
(man) to give them names.
And each animal that will be named by Adam,
that newly named animal will become nefesh
chayah ("a living soul.") And Adam named all the
animals, the birds of the sky and the beasts of
the field, but no spouse was found for Adam.

As will be later discussed, the act of naming or renaming in the Bible is an act of a verbal creation, since once a person is renamed (Sarai turns into Sarah, Abram turns into Abraham, and Jacob turns into Israel), that person is uplifted and placed on an elevated pedestal of humanity and piety.

Hence, when God directs Adam/man to name the animals, Adam/man turns into a creator, a verbal creator. As already mentioned, when Adam/man names all the animals, one reads that by naming an animal, it will become *nefesh chayah,* a "living soul." It further stresses Adam's /man's elevated status as a verbal creator.

However, one must keep in mind that the major reason for naming the animals by Adam/man is to enable Adam/man to observe all animals and find among them a spouse/mate for himself. The latter is stressed by the following two assumptions. First, God creates all those animals only after He realizes that Adam/man will do much better with a spouse/mate next to him. Accordingly, there is a causal connection between Adam's naming the animals and God's expecting him to find among the animals the right spouse/mate for himself. Therefore, naming the animals is indeed a tool to be used by Adam/ man to select one of the named animals as a spouse/mate.

Second, one reads that God created all the animals "from earth." The latter brings to mind that also Adam/ man was created "from earth" (Genesis, 2,7). Hence, since Adam/man and all the animals were created from the very same "raw material," carved from the very same "quarry," it is nothing but a given and logical to assume that once Adam/man finds among the animals a spouse/mate, he will make the right choice.

Nevertheless, all those expectations gradually built and cultivated are frustrated and breached. It says that after the animals parade in front of Adam/man, after making quite clear that one of the animals will be the right choice to become a spouse/mate for Adam/man (as both Adam and the animals had been created from the same "raw material" from the same "quarry")—that paragraph ends with the concluding statement that God did not find among the animals a right spouse/mate for Adam/man.

From the artistic perspective, therefore, the reader experiences frustrated expectations. He/she was strongly encouraged to build and cultivate one kind of expecta- tions, but the latter are surprisingly breached and denied. This is an aesthetic-rhetorical device that causes the reader to unearth and comprehend the latent ideological/ moral message inlaid in this short story: since Adam/man is the verbal creator of the animals, he cannot choose one of them as a spouse/mate. As a verbal creator of the animals, Adam/man is above the animals and therefore, no animal is suitable for him as his spouse/mate. Breach- ing the latter is both existentially and morally wrong.

Literary Devices and Mechanisms

The aesthetic mechanism that consists of a rhetorical device of frustrated expectations (which yields a surprise) serves effectively the latent ideological/moral message inlaid in that text.

The last example is the following, taken from the flood story in the book of Genesis (chapters 6-9). Indeed, it is a very well-known story about the moral righteousness of Noah that saved him (and his family and the chosen animals) from the devastating flood. The following discussion aims to prove—through the operation of an aesthetic device—that that public knowledge calls for an adjustment."

Here is the way in which Noah is introduced to the reader for the very first time. This introduction consists of three statements.

1) "This is the line of Noah."

2) "Noah was a righteous man in his generation; Noah walked with God."

3) "Noah begot three sons, Shem, Ham and Japheth."

"Formally," the righteousness of Noah, according to the way in which it is introduced to the reader, is absolutely flawless. Hence, in a generation of heartless sinners, Noah was the only righteous person.

However, once the reader follows carefully the evolving nature of the textual sequence, does he/she realize that there is something "wrong" in the way that Noah is introduced. Accordingly, once the first phrase shares with the reader that "this is the line of Noah," the reader justly cultivates expectations that the following phrase will portray in detail the "line of Noah," his "family tree."

Those expectations are breached and frustrated, however. Instead of continuing with the line of Noah, instead of fulfilling the text's "promise," the text focuses in considerable detail on the perfect righteousness of Noah. Thus, the natural reaction of the reader to the second statement is the following: with all due respect to the blameless righteousness of Noah, we were promised to be acquainted with the line of Noah; we cultivated expectations in light of the latter, but our expectations were denied and frustrated.

From the artistic/aesthetic perspective, that text practices in this case a rhetorical device of frustrated expectations: the text "promised" the reader to share with him/her a certain type of information, and that "promise" is broken. What you see is not what you get. In this case, what you were promised, you neither see nor get. Thus the reader is in position of asking the following: Why did the text encourage me to cultivate a specific kind of expectations and later breach those expectations? What does the text earn from that act of "leading astray"?

The answer seems to be associated with one word only: generation (*bedoratav*). Noah was a righteous person "in his generation." Why does the text add the word "generation"? Hence it is a logical given that Noah could be righteous only in his generation since he did not live in another generation. Noah could not be righteous in the generation of Abraham or of Moses, since their generations lived thousands of years after Noah's generation. The latter brings back the question: Why does the text add the unnecessary, questionable word "generation," while the introduced information/text could do much better without that addition?

It seems that there is only one way to resolve that "enigmatic" question. Since Noah's generation was a generation of atrocious sinners, perhaps it was not so difficult, or so challenging, to be considered righteous in such a generation. Perhaps even a very ordinary person could be easily considered a righteous person in such a sinful generation.

Only after breaching the reader's expectations does the textual continuum provide with the suspended information regarding the line of Noah: "Noah begot three sons: Shem, Ham, and Japheth."

Hence, the text amalgamates two aesthetic devices to deliver the latent moral message. The first aesthetic device is a compositional device, since it is associated with the order of presentation, the compositional way in which the text is organized. That order is "illogical" and causes the breach of expectations. The second aesthetic device is rhetorical, while stemming from the compositional device: the rhetorical device consists of frustrated expectations (surprise) and that aesthetic device was practically "conceived" by the compositional device. The two aesthetic devices—compositional and rhetorical—are causally tied to each other while delivering the latent moral message of the text: Noah was not as righteous as it has been generally believed for "countless" generations.

The next question is the following: Why does the text aim to partially belittle the righteousness of Noah? The answer to this question seems to be found in the following chapter, chapter 9. Noah drank wine, became intoxicated and shamefully exposed his intimate parts in his tent. Hence, such a person cannot be portrayed as a flawless righteous person. Although he did not commit a transgression, his behavior was very far from being acceptable as the most righteous person upon earth.

Therefore, the text prudently "enlists" two aesthetic devices that are causally connected to each other in order to support and deliver the text's latent moral message.

The following chapters of the book further demonstrate how the biblical text cleverly weaves its tales and stories while interlacing in them aesthetic mechanisms to convey the latent ideological (liturgical, moral, historical, social) message of the text.

PSALM 23:
THE LORD IS MY SHEPHERD ...
OR IS HE MY HOST?

The grace and the power of the 23rd Psalm have always captured the critics' attention and spurred them to seek the source of these qualities. But though the critics have been impressed by the psalm's lyrical appeal, they have found its composition perplexing, even disturbing. The sharp transition from the shepherd-sheep metaphor to the host-guest metaphor may seem awkward, upsetting the psalm's coherence.

Some have attempted to uncover the psalm's unity by philological interpretation or language emendation. Others have suggested that the psalm's bisected composition should be tolerated in light of its remarkable aesthetics and message, both of which fully compensate for its loose organization.

The psalm's unity is likely manifested in the text in its present form, but too, we may find the secret of the psalm's dynamic unity in the interaction of its two metaphor clusters. The decisive literary phenomena in the psalm are its metaphor patterns and its composition. The psalm begins with the metaphor "The Lord is my shepherd" (*Yahweh ro'i*) and elaborates it until it resembles in scope an epic simile in which the tenor seems to be abandoned, while the vehicle is developed independently: "He makes me lie down in green pastures; He leads me beside still waters; He restores my soul" (verses 1-3).

The culmination of the shepherd-sheep imagery leads the reader to expect more of the same. Such paratactic patterns require something external to break their momentum and bring them to closure. The hemistich "for His name's sake" does this, playing the role of *deus ex machina*, disturbing the momentum of the imagery, while yet propelling the psalm toward its conclusion. Suddenly, we emerge from the metaphor and leave the first paratactic sequence ready for something new.

This rhetorical technique of violated expectations is not part of the metaphorical development alone. It also serves as the psalm's ideology. The phrase "for His name's sake" shifts our attention from the believer—who is the focus of the previous phrases—to God. In this way, the author prevents the believer's role from overshadowing God's. This rhetorical-ideological stratagem is supported by another literary device that may be called "textual circularity."

The phrase, "For His name's sake" thematically resembled the opening of the psalm, "The Lord is ...," as it also makes God the focus of attention. Opening and closing the unit with analogous elements evoke a sense of circularity and demarcate the unit. By drawing our attention back to God, this circularity compensates for the previous concentration on the believer. Subsequently, the believer is allowed to be the focus of attention without overshadowing God's role.

Psalm 23

The second literary system that plays a significant role in molding the aesthetics of Psalm 23 may be called "dynamic metaphorical evolution." The opening metaphor of the psalm, "The Lord is my shepherd..." (*Yahweh ro'i*) depicts God as a shepherd and the believer as a sheep. This keeper-animal figuration is extended: "He makes me to lie down in green pastures; He leads me beside still waters." But the process of animal-like figuration is disturbed by a thematic deviation: "He restores my soul" (*nafshi yeshovev*). The thematic concentration upon the believer's soul—the most distinguishing characteristic of human beings—shifts the attention from animal to human characteristics.

This shift is echoed by alliteration, as *nafshi yeshovev* produces a significant sound pattern (based on the repetition of f/v/s), which shifts from the psalm's preceding alliterative trail. The animal figuration is weakened and gradually diminished by an increasing emphasis on the believer's human characteristics. To be sure, one may argue that the soul (*nefesh*) is not less animal-like than human, since its detonation refers to all living things (see Job 12:10, *nefesh kol chai* [the soul of every living thing]; Gen. 1:30; and others). Yet, the fact that *nefesh* most often designates human beings (Gen. 36:6, *nafshot beto* [people of his house]; Exod. 12:4, *nefashot* [people]; Exod. 1:5, [all the people (*nefesh*) who came out of Jacob's loins, seventy people]) brings *nefesh*'s connotation closer to humans' characteristics than to an animal's.

Although the animal-like figuration is not dropped, the animal characteristics gradually fade, while the human characteristics are emphasized. This metaphorical evolution reaches its peak at the psalm's climactic conclusion, where the believer completely drops the animal-like figuration and is elevated to an exclusively human figuration: "Surely goodness and mercy shall follow me all the days of my life; and I shall dwell in the house of the Lord forever."

The gradual metamorphosis of the animal figuration into a human one (begun in v. 3 [*nafshi yeschovev*] evolves in the verse's continuation: "He guides me in straight paths/circles ..." The expression "straight paths" (*ma'gley tzedek*) [righteousness]) advances the metaphorical evolution: the word "righteousness" is exclusively in the domain of human beings. Only human beings, not animals, may be judged by criteria of righteousness, because that attribute derives from a moral choice and an intellectual discrimination, possessed by humans only.

Therefore, using the concept of righteousness (*tzedek*) at this stage of the figurative metamorphosis strengthens the human characteristics of the sheep metaphor, while simultaneously contributing to the fading of the animal figuration.

As the animal figuration fades, it is not completely dismissed. The expression *yancheni* (will guide me) is syntactically engaged with *ma'gley* (paths/circles) and both are still permeated with animal-like characteristics. The word *ma'gley*, "paths," literally means "circles." The root a.g.l., from which *ma'gley* derives, appears in many places in the Bible, meaning "circle" (Proverbs 2;9; Psalms 4;11, Psalms 1;20, and others).

The common translation of *ma'gley* as "paths" is certainly valid. That word often refers to a man's way in his life's course (Psalms 65;2; Psalms 2;9; Proverbs 4;26). Yet the etymological connotation origin of "circle" is evidently heard in *ma'gley*; it gives rise to connotations of a labor routine of a domestic animal, working for man and guided and goaded by him. Thus, the animal figuration of the shepherd-sheep metaphor echoes still.

The figurative metamorphosis continues: "Yea, though I walk through the valley of the shadow of death / I will fear no evil." On the one hand, the gradual development of the metaphorical dynamics is accelerated in this verse. The frightening picture of walking in a somber valley reinforces the human characteristics of the image, because it relates to humans walking along paths of perils and traps, physical as well as mental and emotional.

On the other hand, the roaming in the valley still reminds us of the wandering sheep, and consequently does not let the animal figuration drop, although it is a gradual process of fading away.

The same process is repeated in the following hemistich: "Your rod and staff, they comfort me." The rod (*shevet*) and the staff (*mishantecha*) refer to implements a shepherd uses in guiding his sheep. Though the human characteristics of the sheep metaphor increase in this hemistich—"comfort" [*yenachamuni*] suits human nature much better than animal—the reference to the rod presents and consequently preserves the animal-like figuration.

Verse 5 begins with the host metaphor ("You prepare a table before me...") and designates a turning point in the process of the dynamic metaphorical development. As the host-guest metaphor begins, the shepherd-sheep metaphor is abandoned. The new metaphorical scene of host and guest completely exposes the latent human characteristics. Now we can see that the first impression of compositional looseness in the psalm is nothing but a delusion. The ending metaphor (of animal-like characteristics) but plausibly evolves from it through a gradual process of figurative metamorphosis:

A. The gradual metamorphosis within the shepherd metaphor

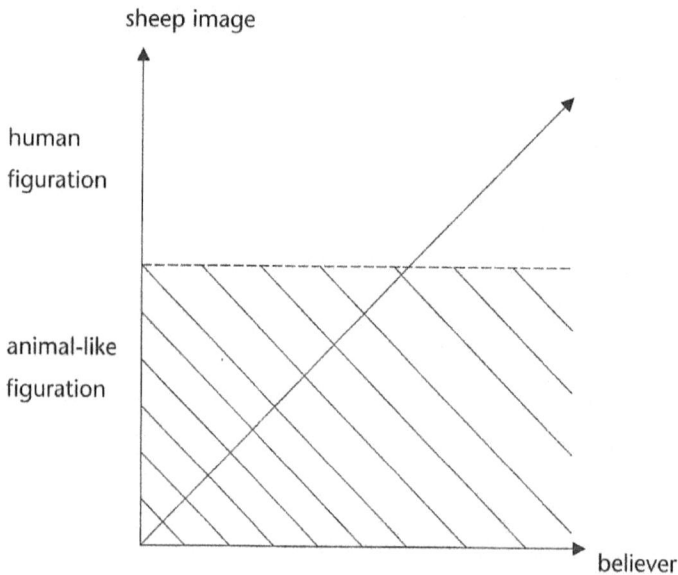

B. The gradual integration between the psalm's two predominant metaphors

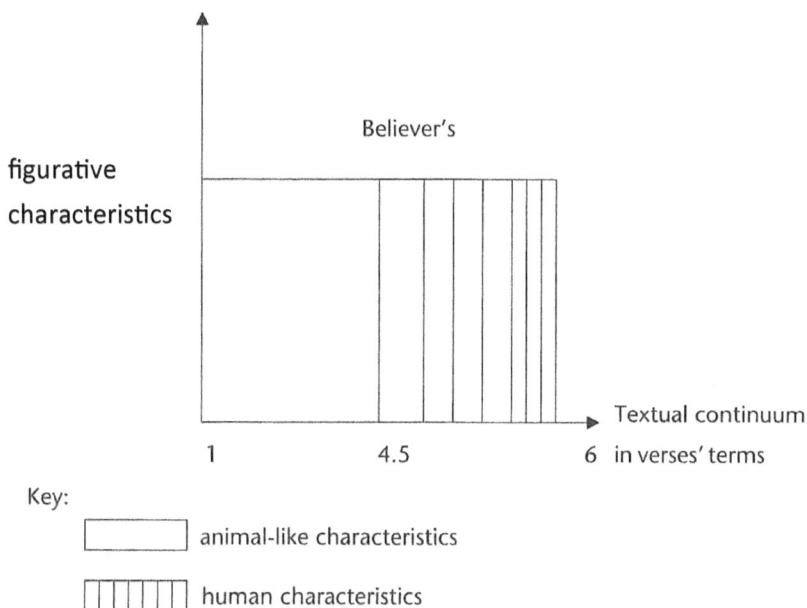

Key:

| | animal-like characteristics |
| | human characteristics |

The movement in the focus of attention from the believer to God in the first system partially discloses the shift from animal to human figuration in the second. In both cases, there is a shift from a lower to a higher spiritual level. The difference in the nature of the shifts—a sudden shift in the first system, as opposed to a gradual shift in the second system—is of considerable rhetorical merit. It moderates and softens the precise parallelism's rigidity, and subsequently grants the psalm a sense of authentic flexibility. Thus, the Lord is the believer's host no less than his shepherd. The two metaphors that seemed to be in conflict are indeed logically interlocked and convey an integrated picture of God's dual grace: the stern protector and the generous host.

WHO IS AFRAID OF AN INTELLECTUAL WOMAN? THE WOMAN, THE MAN, AND THE SERPENT IN THE GARDEN OF EDEN

In Genesis 3, the woman is doubly deprived. First, the woman—Eve—is shortchanged intellectually. The narrator, inspired by the implied author, does not or cannot accept that the female is intellectually superior to the male; he applies several ingenious aesthetic devices to trip her up and put in question her intellectual faculties.

Then we discern that the woman is also maltreated on the sexual level. In the story of temptation, she is presented as the instigator, the beguiler. Therefore, the woman's deprivation is two-fold: the sexual and intellectual dispositions are linked, the former giving rise to the latter.

The narrator of the next example of aesthetics of chastisement (Genesis 3;6), enlists the best of poetic abilities as he scolds Eve for disobeying God's command and eating the forbidden fruit. This case, however, differs somewhat from previous examples, in that the criticism here is not entirely justified. On the one hand, Eve merits criticism (as does Adam) for challenging God's restriction and His divine command. On the other hand, while Eve deserves criticism on moral grounds, she does not deserve to be scolded on an intellectual basis. It is Eve, not Adam, who displays curiosity and who is tantalized by the idea that she might possess the divine knowledge that only God possesses.

It is evident that Eve is tempted not on sensual grounds, but only on an intellectual basis: the only reason that drives her to eat the fruit from the Tree of Knowledge is the serpent's promise that she will gain divine knowledge. This underlines the fact that Eve cannot resist the thought that she might acquire knowledge shared only by God. Indeed, the serpent's promise that Eve would not die if she touched the forbidden tree further goaded her to taste its fruit.

However, this does not negate the fact that Eve's only motivation in eating the forbidden fruit was purely intellectual. She wanted to know. Eve's claim to intellectual power is further substantiated when she, not Adam, speaks out, demonstrating verbal skill, which is one of the most salient manifestations of intellectual capacity.

Despite the fact that God bestowed Adam with verbal superiority (by making him name all living creatures, including woman), Adam does not utter a word, but Eve proves articulate. In this context, one can discern the narrator's scolding aimed at Adam. Though he supposedly possesses verbal superiority, he is mute and speaks out only when God addresses him directly, and then only to incriminate his wife for an act in which he was a full participant.

Neither Adam's silence nor his eventual speech earns him much respect. The narrator's version of Genesis 3:6 chides Adam on intellectual grounds for failing to exercise his verbal capacity, and on character flaws as well (he

proves to be a coward who tries to escape blame by incriminating his wife). Although the narrator's principle criticism is reserved for Eve and not for Adam, her transgression should neither cloud nor belittle her intellectual faculties. The narrator enlists an intricate literary system that joins three aesthetic devices to cast a shadow on Eve's intellectual powers.

The fact that God wished to bestow verbal superiority on Adam is connected with the narrator's latent criticism of Eve on intellectual grounds. Indeed, the narrator does not do justice to Eve in belittling her intellectual faculties.

As in criticizing Abraham, the narrator of Genesis 3;6 repeats the literary device of utilizing the context, while combining it with a comprehensive rhetorical mechanism of critical aesthetics of chastisement. Fifteen verses earlier, the narrator reports the amazing task God gives Adam, that of naming all living creatures on earth (Genesis 2;19-20). Adam completes this task, finishing by naming woman (Genesis 2;23). Naming all living creatures demonstrates Adam's intellectual superiority over all creatures, including woman, and points out the irony when Eve speaks up.

When Adam finally does talk, his words are far from flattering to his humanity (Genesis 3;12). First, he blames the woman for a sin that he shares. Secondly, the act of naming in the Bible carries connotations of creation ("The world was created by a word" [*haOlam nivra beMilah*] is a well-known Rabbinic adage) and of new birth.

Such is the case when God renames Abram and Sarai as Abraham and Sarah (in later Judaism, the letter *h* [*heh*] designates God), and when the celestial messenger renames Jacob Israel (after Jacob proved his mettle in the struggle with God's angel), as the Hebrew etymology attests.

Thus, naming all living creatures made Adam a partner in God's creation: his verbal creations completed God's concrete creations. The Hebrew text reinforces the creative function connected with Adam's naming the living creatures: "and whatever Man will name it, living soul is its name." This seemingly clumsy syntax is particularly significant: once Man names an animal, the animal earns life and turns into a "living soul" (*nefesh chaya*). Thus naming truly equals creation.

But, scolding Eve (at that time, she is still called *Isha* [woman]) while stressing Adam's intellectual-verbal superiority proves a shrewd literary device on the part of the narrator, who wishes to lessen the woman's intellectual qualities that prompted her to disobey God. The context is an effective tool in conveying latent criticism. While Eve deserves criticism on moral grounds for disobeying God, her intellect does not merit criticism. The fact that intellectual curiosity made Eve sin on moral/religious grounds probably makes the narrator do her the injustice of denigrating her intellectual acumen. Using the context as a critical tool is just part of the narrator's latent, intricate system of (wrongly) criticizing Eve on intellectual grounds.

The narrator first insinuates that it is the physical, rather than intellectual, attractions of the forbidden fruit that tempted Eve. Then he reports that she confuses the names of the two trees in the Garden of Eden. In Genesis 2;9, we read that the full name of the Tree of Life is "the Tree of Life in the middle of the garden"; the full name of the Tree of Knowledge is "The Tree of Knowledge of Good and Evil." But in Genesis 3;3, when Eve speaks with the serpent and refers to the forbidden tree (the Tree of Knowledge), she mistakenly refers to it as the "tree in the middle of the garden," the name of the Tree of Life.

Eve seems to confuse the names of the two trees, which might have been her own fault. However, the narrator's ascribing the wrong words to Eve is part of his shrewd, unfair attempt to discredit her on an intellectual-verbal basis, in order to belittle her intellectual abilities. Intellectuality is conditioned by verbal faculties. The third stage in the narrator's attack on Eve makes his second phase more evident.

As previously stated, Eve is attracted to the Tree of Knowledge on purely intellectual grounds. The serpent makes two promises when he tempts Eve to try the fruit of the Tree of Knowledge: 1) that she will gain immortality, and 2) that the fruit will bestow on her divine knowledge possessed only by God. The attraction of the first promise certainly tempts Eve, but it has no effect on the purely intellectual nature of the second promise, which concerns only intellect and does not even hint at sensual pleasure.

Who's Afraid of an Intellectual Woman?

Although Eve's intellectual curiosity was probably aroused prior to her encounter with the serpent, that encounter finally drove her to satisfy that curiosity. Thus, it was only Eve's intellectual faculties that made her breach the word of God. Now, the narrator deviates from this when he names the three reasons that were the grounds for Eve's attraction to the Tree of Knowledge: "And woman saw that (a) the tree was good for eating, (b) and a delight to the eyes, and (c) that the tree was desirable as a source of knowledge or wisdom, she took of its fruit and ate" (Genesis 3;6).

The narrator's rhetorical deceit is so effective that none of the commentators or biblical scholars who studied Genesis has ever doubted its accuracy. The narrator who aims to conceal Eve's intellectual motivation in being attracted to the Tree of Knowledge attributes to her two clearly sensual motivations, while delaying the third—intellectual motivation—to the end of the list and presenting it in a sensual context.

The use of the Hebrew word *ta'vah* (delight), which also means lust and sexual passion, in the context of *ta'vah laeinayim* (delight to the eyes), underlines the sensual drives that the narrator tries to attribute unfairly to Eve. Although he grudgingly offers the third motivation as well (the promise of knowledge), he still manages to anchor it in the context of sexual passion, to lessen any intellectualism connected with that motivation.

The narrator states that Eve realized that the tree was *nechmad lehaskil*—desirable as a source of knowledge (wisdom). Since *nechmad* derives from the Hebrew root *ch.m.d*, which designates lust or sexual passion, its appearance in the context of *lehaskil* (to impart knowledge) considerably reduces any claim to intellectualism, and therefore Eve's wish to acquire intellectual knowledge is seemingly motivated by nothing more than a low sensual passion. Also, the word *lehaskil* (to acquire knowledge) is pushed to the very rear of the phrase, while almost disarming it of its intellectual essence (a compositional device).

The narrator thus enlists two aesthetic devices (attributing sensual motivations to Eve, and anchoring her intellectual motivation in a sensual context), based on theme and composition, in order to belittle her intellectual motivation.

Moreover, to mislead the reader and leave the impression that Eve's temptation was brought about by an erotic quest, not an intellectual one, the narrator strews the story with erotic allusions: the injunction against sexual contact between humans and animals, the sexual union of man and woman (*basar echad*, meaning one flesh) the suggestive phallic shape of the serpent, and the fact that the knowledge acquired by Adam and Eve is sexual, carnal knowledge. Before tasting the forbidden fruit, "they were both naked, the man and his wife, and were not ashamed (Genesis 4;25).

After eating the fruit of the Tree of Knowledge, they possess sexual awareness, which engenders shame, "and their eyes were opened, and they knew they were naked, and they sewed fig leaves together, and made themselves aprons" (Genesis 3;7). It is a matter of considerable interest that the serpent is *arum* (shrewd, the one who conceals his intentions), while man and woman are *arumyim* (naked, concealing nothing).

The narrator's effort to denigrate Eve and discount her intellectual capabilities is reflected also in his attitude toward Eve and Lot's wife. It should be noted, as far as names are concerned, that the Bible ascribes much higher verbal and intellectual abilities to Adam than to his wife. By naming and defining the woman, Adam seems to verbally create her. He names her twice: woman (Genesis 2;23) and then Eve (Genesis 3;20). In Hebrew, Eve's name is *Chava*, which derives from *chayim*, life. The woman's

identity is thus partially erased, and she is inextricably linked to Adam.

As previously noted, Lot's wife suffers from similar discrimination. Like Eve, Lot's wife disobeys God's command out of intellectual curiosity and is duly punished. Lot's wife breaches God's command, looks back due to her desire to know what devastation God has wrought ("But his wife looked back behind him, and she became a pillar of salt" (Genesis 19;26).

While Eve is diminished when she is given a name (being defined in relation to man and from his perspective), Lot's wife does not even deserve a name; she is referred to only as "Lot's wife." And then she is sentenced to death.

THE BIBLE AND SEXUAL EXPLOITATION: THE CASE OF SARAH

The way Sarah is portrayed and treated is representative; it serves as a test case, wherein all the manifestations of biblical women's maltreatment and the biblical narrator's antifeminist attitudes are amalgamated.

First, Sarah is "sold" by the male (Abraham, her own husband and God's chosen herald, the forefather of the Hebrew/Israelite/Jewish nation!) as "sexual merchandise." Abraham sells to the Egyptians, and eventually the Pharaoh, Sarah's sexual services to gain entrance to Egypt and improve his financial situation. Sarah is not only deprived of her personal freedom, but also of her elementary rights as an independent human being.

Similarly, the biblical narrator (who is a mouthpiece of the implied author and his ideology) robs Sarah of the ability to express her own feelings and voice her opinion when Isaac, her beloved son, to whom she gave birth after long years of agony and frustration, is about to be killed.

A male-dominated society delivered to Sarah a clear and cruel message: without children, without a fertile womb, she is nothing, she has no importance as a human being. No wonder that Sarah is willing to surrender her self-respect and to give up her intimacy with her husband, when she gives him her servant Hagar, to act on her behalf as a surrogate mother, as a womb for hire. Sarah seems to have accepted and internalized the cruel social dictates of her male-dominated society. As a result, Sarah tries to compensate for her failure to give her husband a child and prevent him from divorcing her and leaving her destitute. The Bible, being male-oriented, fails to consider the possibility that the man might be the infertile one. (Barren Rachel did the very same upon giving her female servant Bilha to her husband Jacob to conceive a child.)

Sarah has no value from the biblical perspective; she is the embodiment of the Latin adage, *tolla mulier in utero*—a woman is nothing but a womb. These observations about Sarah's and Rachel's situation apply to too many women in the Bible.

Sexual Exploitation and the Entrapment of Women

The first example of cynical sexual exploitation is the sale of Sarah by her husband Abraham as a piece of sexual merchandise to improve his financial situation. (Indeed, at this early stage of Abraham's unfolding chronicles his name is still Abram.) Genesis 12;10-20 narrates Abraham and Sarah's (here she is still called Sarai) descent to the land of Egypt because of a famine in the land of Canaan.

All the early scholars who addressed this chronicle commented on Abraham's questionable conduct: not only does Abraham lie in asking Sarah to pretend that she is his sister, he also informs Sarah that she may have to pay a sexual price so that "it may be well with me on account of you and my soul shall live thanks to you."

While most of the commentators and biblical scholars have attempted to reason Abraham's sins on legalistic-formal grounds, the biblical narrator sardonically and sarcastically scolds Abraham on moral grounds. Despite the fact that the narrator's criticism is introduced subtly, through a dense cluster of literary devices, his rebuking voice is clear and strongly ironic.

Interestingly enough, while modern scholars ignore Abraham's questionable morality and instead discuss legal technicalities of the Ancient Near East, the 13th-century commentator Nahmanides (Rabbi Moshe ben Nahman) openly condemns Abraham. Nevertheless, Nahmanides does not rebuke Abraham on moral grounds, but rather on the basis of pious faith: Abraham should have *trusted* God to extricate him from misfortune and should not have lied about Sarah's marital status.

While the majority of commentators and scholars have overlooked Abraham's disturbing morality that led him to offer his wife's sexual services, not only to save his own life, but also to make a profit, the biblical narrator has a totally different reaction. His chastisement is aesthetically sophisticated and equally forceful; the fact that it may have gone unnoticed until now is no reflection on its force and merit. How has this aesthetic sophistication managed to remain undiscovered for so long? The narrator, in an impressive display of poetic skill, groups eight(!) literary devices into one harmonious system that effectively expresses the sarcastic, sardonic chastisement and criticism aimed at Abraham.

The first literary device is the chastisement context. The narrator centers his report on Abraham's sin in the context of Abraham's decent from Canaan, the Promised Land. The famine in Canaan is hardly a good reason for leaving the Promised Land, particularly when God Himself assures Abraham that He will make Abraham a great nation (*goy gadol*). In Genesis 12;1, God notifies Abraham that He has given him the Promised Land and tells Abraham to move there. In verse 4, Abraham follows God's command and goes to the Promised Land. In verse 5, Abraham arrives in the Promised Land, and five verses later, he deserts the Promised Land.

The argument that Abraham left because of a famine is both true and false, although archeological data prove that there was a famine in Canaan, but not all the inhabitants chose to leave. Abraham, who was an affluent tribal leader and presumably had at his disposal all the privileges associated with such a rank, did choose to leave. The narrator uses the verb root *y.r.d.* (descended). This choice is neither random nor arbitrary, for it expresses all the negative connotations associated with "descent," to go down.

Abraham proves himself too hasty when he leaves the Promised Land, given to him by God, not for reasons of survival, but for purely economic motives. Abraham's shameful departure from the Promised Land parallels his equally shameful conduct in heading for Egypt.

In the narrator's eyes, Abraham could indeed have remained in Canaan and survived the famine with little or no difficulty due to his status. His subsequent behavior—namely the selling of his wife's sexual services in Egypt—

becomes less the action of a desperate man trying to survive and more the action of a man trying to gain economic or material benefits and is, as such, open to negative comment.

The second literary device is the following: The critical narrator adds that Abraham left the Promised Land for Egypt to dwell (*lagur*) there. What might the reason be for such an unnecessary addition. To stress the undeniable fact that Abraham did desert the Promised Land. (This second literary device is also of thematic nature.)

Although many who have examined this case conclud-
ed that Abraham's questionable behavior was a matter of
survival (he sacrificed his wife's honor and body on the
altar of her husband's life), the validity of this argument
seems as questionable as Abraham's conduct. Was it truly
a matter of life and death on the part of Abraham? Did
anyone actually force him to leave Canaan and cross the
Egyptian border?

As we know, Abraham was a wealthy and influential
man who certainly could have remained in Canaan (as did
others) and suffered little or no hardship. Apparently,
then, it was economic and materialistic concerns that
motivated Abraham, rather than survival.

The reader may deduce all this from the censorious
tone of the narrator, who criticizes Abraham's materialistic
action through the careful use of words and impressive
aesthetic dexterity. Perhaps we may never know exactly
what crossed Abraham's mind when he asked his wife to
pretend that she was his sister, we may certainly deduce
that if the Egyptians had known that Sarah was Abraham's wife, they probably would have killed him and taken
her (Genesis 12;12-13). If they suspected she was his
sister, they would have been more likely to pay him
handsomely for her, in which case, he would not only
survive, but possibly receive something extra as well.

Abraham must have realized this, so the questions
remain: Why did he leave Canaan? Why did he not stop at
the Egyptian border, while realizing that he would have to
sell his wife—for good!) as sexual merchandise? Why did
he not forgo the wealth of Egypt purchased with his wife's
sexual services?

The narrator leads the reader to surmise, through indirect criticism, that Abraham most likely could have avoided this entire situation, yet did not. In his implicit criticism of Abraham, the narrator's *"j'accuse"* subtly paints a picture of a man who leaves the Promised Land after a divine promise that he will become a great nation in the Promised Land, who goes in search of easy wealth and who sells his wife's sexual services in an attempt to gain material profit and perhaps preserve his own life, a situation he could have easily avoided by remaining in the Promised Land.

The fact that Abraham's descent from the Promised Land *could have been avoided* (the implication by the narrator is that it *should* have been avoided) combines with the fact that he evidently left solely to gain material wealth.

The third literary device used by the narrator materializes when he reports that Abraham asks Sarah to pretend that she is his sister: *lema'n itav li ba'avourech* (in order that it may be well with me). As the narrator frames the incriminating story of Abraham's questionable conduct within the context of his descent from the Promised Land, the story, with its message of chastisement, is effectively emphasized. We encounter Abraham's questionable conduct after having learned of his descent from the Promised Land, and the reader is more alert to Abraham's next sin.

The fourth literary device the narrator uses in his subtle aesthetics of chastisement is also thematic. Since all informational data supplied by the textual continuum can be classified as thematic, the fact that the narrator

enables Abraham to verbalize his selfish argument (*lema'n itav li ba'avourech*) can be considered a thematic literary device, as well as critical rhetoric. Abraham's argument, "in order that it may be well with me" further incriminates him, as it reflects his selfish desire for material gain, deriving from indifference to his wife's well-being.

The fifth literary device used by the narrator is compositional, namely, the order of presentation of the thematic materials along the unfolding text. Abraham formulates two supportive arguments for asking his wife to pretend she is his sister: (1) *lema'n itav li ba'avourech* (that it may be well with me because of you), and (2) *wechayta nafshi biglalech* (I may remain alive thank to you).

The coexistence of the two arguments is further stressed because they are constructed as two analogous components within one poetic parallelism (a characteristic of biblical poetry). Each of the arguments is based upon three metrical stresses, and each of them ends with the same rhyme (*ba'avourech, biglalech*), all of which strengthens the impression that the two sequential arguments resemble two analogous components (hemistiches) fused into one poetic equation (parallelism). The reader is guided to treat the two sequential arguments equally, while noting that despite their formal affinity (on the grounds of syntax, meter, and sound pattern), they differ dramatically in content.

Correspondingly, while the first argument is concerned with material benefit, the second is concerned with survival. The shrewd narrator, in an effort to subtly convey his condemnation of Abraham, reverses the logical order of the two arguments, beginning with the materialistic argument and delaying presentation of the more urgent one, staying alive. Consequently, the narrator sheds a sarcastic light on Abraham's conduct: Abraham is presented as a materialistic person whose prime interest is to be bountifully rewarded, while his second argument is mere lip service, claiming that his life is in serious danger.

The literary-compositional device thus proves effective: the order of presentation is neither a random syntactical structure, nor does it echo an "indifferent structural container," into which the content is poured and framed. The order of presentation is a clever compositional literary device, skillfully enlisted by an able narrator to convey disapproval.

The sixth literary device, of thematic-rhetorical nature, is founded upon textual repetition. Again, we see that Abraham introduces his selfish argument in the following stylistic fashion: *lema'n itav li ba'avourech* (that it may be well with me because of you). The narrator echoes the same verbal pattern when he refers to the successful outcome of Abraham's plot: *uleAbram heytiv ba'avourah* (and because of her, it went well with Abraham). This verbal, echoing repetition stresses that Abraham's materialistic plot succeeded and yielded the exact result Abraham had planned and desired. The narrator's use of the same formula reveals yet another critical arrow aimed at the Patriarch. What Abraham greedily desired and planned for, he got—at the expense of his wife.

The seventh literary device is both thematic and rhetorical. After informing the reader of the success of Abraham's plan, the narrator goes into a surprising amount of detail, listing the valuables Abraham receives from Pharaoh in payment for Sarah's services: "and he [Abraham] acquired herds of sheep and cattle, and asses, and slaves, and maidservants, and she-asses, and camels" (Genesis 12;16). Not only is this list long, it is further lengthened by the use of the conjunctive *waw* (and).

One of the most distinctive characteristics of the biblical text is its concise and economical use of words. But the narrator in this particular case deviates from the norm in detailing a lengthy list of presents, which really does not have much to do with the chronicle. Thus, the obtrusiveness of the list, which seems almost clumsily grafted onto the unfolding tale, is a deliberate rhetorical signpost (one might call it rhetorical "bait"), which draws the reader's attention by piquing his curiosity.

In purposely calling the reader's attention to the list, the narrator causes the reader to become more alert and sensitive to the narrator's latent criticism. In the same manner, the reader realizes that the narrator has purposely drawn his attention to the long list of gifts, thus ironically emphasizing Abraham's materialistic plan and how handsomely he was rewarded for his wife's sexual services.

The eighth literary device is also thematic. It is a matter of much interest that once Sarah is sold to the Pharaoh, her name is not mentioned anymore, as she is now called *isha* (woman). Hence, her identity was stolen from her, erased, when she became a piece of (sexual) merchandise.

Although the narrator never openly utters a single word of direct criticism against Abraham, he conveys his censure and scathing scorn in a powerful, albeit indirect, manner. The aesthetics of chastisement in the Bible assume, in this case, an impressive artistry. The narrator

manages to orchestrate a ramified, intricate array of literary devices, which he operates in order to express sharp criticism of Abraham, without upsetting the surface impression of an objective and unobtrusive report. That the narrator's chastisement is not direct does not lessen its effect. And the interpretive excavation that uncovers the narrator's latent criticism is no less important. It not only provides the reader with an "unofficial" perspective of Abraham's conduct, on that the "official" surface text pretends not to possess, it also provides the reader with an excellent opportunity to witness biblical aesthetic artistry at its best.

That and more.

The Bible and Sexual Exploitation: The Case of Sarah

Abraham is considered the laudably, lofty forefather of the Hebrew/Israelite/Jewish people. Indeed, the three great religions—Judaism, Christianity, Islam—are called the Abrahamic religions.

Abraham had two sons. One of them (Ishmael) he "exiled" to an arid, lifeless desert and the second (Isaac) he was about to slaughter. Yet Abraham had earned the "title" as being the most admirable, praiseworthy father through countless generations, in all over the world.

With regard to selling his beloved wife, Sarah, to Pharaoh as sexual merchandise. Undoubtably, Abraham knew "the name of the game": selling Sarah to Pharaoh meant giving her away *for good.* Not only for one night, but forever! Yet that repulsive "sentence," giving away his beloved wife for good, did not stop him. He continued walking, leaving behind his beloved wife to her odious destiny. He let his greed eclipse his human, moral faculties.

Imagine the following: lonely Abraham stays behind in his tent, while his beloved wife, Sarah, is taken to the Pharaoh's palace. Abraham must have known that Pharaoh would have sex with Sarah. How did Abraham feel? What crossed his mind? We don't know.

The only thing we know is that even Sarah's horrendous fate, the one Abraham initiated and orchestrated, did not stop him. He let his greed cloud his mind, mute his good judgment, and eclipse his feelings of caring and compassion.

Indeed, the biblical narrator (conditioned and directed by the story's implied author) does not berate Abraham on solely a moral basis. The narrator rebukes Abraham on a religious basis as well (challenging God's command to sojourn to the Promised Land). The following was already addressed by the biblical narrator: utilizing the linguistic root *y.r.d.* (Abraham *yarad* [went down, descended] to Egypt is "contaminated" by derogatory connotations that scold Abraham for deserting the Promised Land.

However, the narrator's scolding of Abraham for that religious iniquity does not end there. As previously stated, he continues to scold Abraham for that religious transgression by saying the following: "Abraham descended to Egypt *lagur* there, to *dwell and strike roots* in Egypt, a foreign land, a land that is painfully far away from the desirable Promised/Holy Land.

Why did the narrator add the verb *lagur*, to dwell there? Wasn't it enough to write that Abraham went down, descended, to the land of Egypt? Yet adding that word emphasized Abraham's religious transgression, breaking God's command to reside in Canaan, the Holy/Promised Land.

Nevertheless, even the religiously sinful Abraham is still God's chosen prophet. For that reason, the scolding of Abraham is softened by concluding that verse as it commenced, by telling of the famine in Canaan. In this way, the biblical narrator yields the impression that Abraham is "engulfed," is "suffocated" and "besieged" by the famine that justifies his descent from the Holy/Promised Land.

ABRAHAM VERSUS ABRAHAM
THE REAL STORY BEHIND THE STORY
OF THE SACRIFICE OF ISAAC

In the older days of Art,
Builders wrought with greatest care
Each minute and unseen part
For the gods see everywhere.
—H. W. Longfellow, "The Builders"

The story of Isaac's sacrifice (*aqeda*) [binding Isaac to the altar]) seems to be one of the most widely discussed chapters in biblical exegesis. The chronicle of the father, whose profound faith in his God almost led him to sacrifice his beloved son, has been examined from humanistic, theological, psychological, historical, literary, and philosophical standpoints.

The critical tools of the literary approach provides the critic with insight and investigative means to discover new sites in this overly plowed biblical territory. In discussing the rhetorical and compositional layers of the story of Isaac's binding, this chapter also demonstrates that literary devices employed in both rhetoric and composition are there not only for artistic purposes, but also directly link to the foundations of the story, to ideology, theology, and psychology.

As will later be demonstrated, not only one Abraham acts in the *aqeda* story, but rather, there are two conflicting Abrahams: Abraham the loving father and Abraham the pious believer. The conflict between the two Abrahams effectively serves the story's ideological/moral stratum and meritoriously enriches the story's intricate, aesthetic tissue.

Rhetorical Stratagems

The first rhetorical phenomenon is found in the chapter's overture: "And it came to pass after things that God (*ha-Elohim*) did put Abraham to a test and said unto him...Take now your son ... and offer him ... for a burnt offering" (Genesis 22;1-2). By using the word for "did put to a test" (*nisāh*), the narrator shares with the reader crucial information that was denied Abraham. Had Abraham been acquainted with the real intention of the divine command to put him to a test only, the trial would have been robbed of its value.

Thus, an informational gap (which is ironic, because any gap between two levels of awareness produces irony) created by the narrator occurs between Abraham and the reader from the very beginning. The reader, in contrast to Abraham, is able to follow the ensuing chronicle without fear, since he/she expects a happy ending to the story. The menacing features of the story will not intimidate him/her.

On the other hand, the narrator's rhetorical policy of notifying the reader of the happy conclusion of the story at the very beginning seems disturbing and questionable. The rhetorical policy appears to be carried out by an implied author unaware of the rhetorical potential existing in any fictional conclusion, especially one ending a very gripping story.

Instead of cultivating the story's thrilling features to create a suspenseful reading process, the narrator seems to overlook the story's most effective and promising rhetorical potential. But behind this apparent rhetorical misstep, an ideological virtue emerges. While the thrilling plot of the binding (*aqeda*) story has literary merit, it also has an ideological weakness. By capturing the reader's complete attention, the plot may divert attention from the ideological message behind it. A literary cover that is too attractive may eclipse the inner ideological lesson. Thus, once the reader is freed from worrying over the end of the

story, he/she is capable of deciphering the ideological message—Abraham's absolute faith and devotion to God—that emerges from the whole story.

Losing some of the fictional interest enables the ideological lesson to become more obvious, and consequently more effective. The seemingly faulty rhetoric is in fact an effective literary tactic, which adroitly harnesses the rhetorical layer to the ideological purpose.

The second rhetorical stratagem is embedded in the divine command, "... and get thee into the land of Moriah" (v. 2, *lech lecha* [leave, go forth]). This divine command echoes the one opening Genesis 12, "Get thee out of thy country (*lech lecha*) ... unto a land that I will show thee." And again, we read *lech lecha*. The repetition of the most significant components in both commands—*lech lecha*—underlines the analogy between the two commands, and, consequently, reinforces the allusion.

This allusion is a source of both rhetorical and ideological virtues. Although the analogy between the two commands is solid (based upon verbal resemblance and thematic similarity, i.e., extrication from homeland), it still allows a considerable discrepancy between affective connotations.

The divine command in Genesis 12, which ordains Abraham to leave his country for a new one, carries happy connotations, as the new country is the Promised Land—the one in which God will make Abraham a "great nation" (*goy gadol*). The command in Genesis 22, which ordains Abraham to leave his country and go to the Moriah country, is just the opposite. The act Abraham is compelled to commit here has the most horrendous connotations one can imagine.

The disparity in connotation between the two components of the pair of allusions produces an ironic distance that accentuates the somber nature of Abraham's mission at Moriah. The literary-ideological phenomenon demonstrated here is very intricate: it forms an allusion founded upon an analogy, producing a contradictory analogy whose rhetorical impact is ironic and thus ideologically expressive.

One may also discern a rhetorical pattern of unfulfilled expectations. Once the reader identifies the analogy between to two components of the pair of allusions, he/she is expected to assume that the first component in Genesis 12 is auspicious and, consequently, portends the connotative character of the forthcoming component. As the reader reaches the second component in Genesis 22, he/she finds out that the analogy led him/her astray, and his/her optimistic expectations are frustrated.

Denied expectations produce "reverse" reading, as the reader needs to return to previously read information after later information casts a revealing light upon it. This rhetorical pattern of frustrated expectations has an ideological function.

Specifically, the disappointment that results from frustrated expectations sharpens the reader's awareness of the unexpectedly bleak nature of the story of Isaac's binding and consequently reinforces his awareness of Abraham's firm faith.

Composition

The second literary level to be examined is composition. The predominant idea that the psychological and emotional world of the biblical character is obscure and opaque was introduced by previous generations of biblical scholars. The biblical means of characterization cannot be conceived as an opening into the heroes' internal lives, but rather as an opaque barrier. The reader has no knowledge of the heroes' psychological inclinations and motivations, their inner reflections, their doubts.

Erich Auerbach first suggested this particular view of the art of biblical means of characterization in *Mimesis*: "Thoughts and feelings remain unexpressed, are only suggested by the silence of fragmentary speeches." Yet Auerbach's idea about the impenetrable nature of biblical characters' psychogenic lives did not prevail in the field of biblical study. Critics have wisely pointed out that the psychological world of the biblical persona may not be as obscure as one might assume.

The actions of a biblical hero may indeed reflect his thoughts and feelings. Once the critic acquaints himself/herself with the behaviorist code of the biblical persona, he/she is able to solve that character's psychological riddle and decipher his/her psychogenic mechanism. The Bible's evident parsimony in using direct means of psychological characterization is fully compensated for by the usage of indirect means, which enable the reader to enter the recesses of the characters inner life.

An example of the Bible's indirect means of psychological characterization is found in the compositional stratum of the biblical text and may be referred to as the expressive order of presentation. When Abraham is notified by God of the atrocious mission he is expected to carry out, he takes the following steps: "And Abraham rose up early in the morning, and saddled his ass, and took two of his young men with him, and Isaac his son, and clave the wood for the burnt offering, and rose up, and went unto the place of which God had told him" (Genesis 22;3).

Abraham's first act ("rose up early in the morning"), as well as the last ("rose up and went ..."), are certainly both nonconvertible and irreplaceable; any alternative order should start with rising up in the morning and end with leaving. Only the following acts by Abraham are a legitimate matter for alternative orders of presentation: saddled his ass, took two of his young men, took Isaac, clave the wood for the burnt offering. This order of Abraham's acts is undoubtedly one of the many possible sequences. Thus, the biblical author may take the liberty of presenting Abraham's acts in any order to satisfy logical, artistic, and ideological purposes. Rising early in the morning is executed by Abraham, the pious believer (not Abraham, the

Abraham vs. Abraham

loving father), who wishes to fulfill God's command as soon as possible, despite its horrid nature.

In light of this, the question that the critic encounters is: what made the text's implied author choose this order above others? What did he hope to achieve in terms of aesthetics and ideology, by giving up other possibilities of presentation and opting for that particular one? The answer is in the last component of the chosen order, "and [Abraham] clave the wood for a burnt offering." This is the act that most reminds Abraham of the painful mission that he is about to execute.

Since Abraham puts off this emotionally loaded act to the very end, he shows not only a reluctance to obey God's command, but also ambivalence and a powerful inner struggle. Abraham, the loving father, procrastinates as much as possible over the act that reminds him most of his obligation as a believer. The order of presentation proves to be an effective, indirect means of psychological characterization, enabling the reader to break through the seemingly opaque psychogenic world of the biblical character to discover the concealed corners of his mind and heart.

"Everything remains unexpressed," concludes Auerbach in his discussion of the Bible's treatment of feelings. But not quite everything is, in fact, expressed, though differently than we might expect.

The presentational order of Abraham's acts in verse 6 also has an expressive psychological order. "And Abraham took the wood of the burnt offering, and laid it upon Isaac his son; and he took the fire in his hand and a knife." As in the previous order of presentation, the order in this

verse has many possibilities. Abraham's decision to take the knife is delayed to the very last moment. Obviously, taking the knife is the act that foreshadows most tellingly the imminent slaughter. The connotations of devouring and preying implied in the Hebrew word for knife, *ma'chelet* (associated with the verb to eat, to devour), underline the semantic gravity of the knife. Thus the fact that Abraham stalls as much as possible before taking the knife is another example of mobilizing composition for psychological characterization of the seemingly impervious emotional world of the biblical persona.

There are more examples of Isaac's binding story that exhibit the biblical text's tendency to enlist literary devices to portray the emotional and psychological world of the biblical dramatic personae. The first revealing instance is found in the opening of verse 6: "And Abraham took the wood of the burnt offering and laid it upon Isaac his son." Abraham's behavior here, loading his innocent son with the very wood that will consume him, is disturbing indeed. The fact that the biblical narrator refers to Isaac not only by his name but as "his [Abraham's] son" reinforces the emotionally charged atmosphere permeating this verse and sharpens our criticism of Abraham's atrocious act.

A practical explanation for Abraham's astonishing behavior might point out that Abraham was quite old and unable to carry much, whereas Isaac was in the prime of his life. But the validity of this explanation is doubtful since Abraham's physical ability was proven by his three-day journey to Moriah. This explanation also fails in light of the preceding verse (v. 5), which informs us of Abraham's decision to leave the ass behind with the two young men.

If Abraham had burdened Isaac with the wood for the burnt offering for practical reasons, he could certainly have taken at least one ass and loaded it with his heavy wood. That Abraham avoids this practical solution not only stresses his upsetting attitude toward his beloved son, but also sends the reader on an explanatory trail in a direction void of practical nature.

Abraham's seemingly cynical treatment of his son is in fact an expression of his emotional distress, a touching, fatherly attempt to withhold from his well-loved son his woeful fate as long as possible. Abraham, the loving father, is still not ready for Abraham the believer's mission. Once again, he enlists every ruse to delay the execution of his mission.

"Venerable Father Abraham" (as named by Kirkegaard in his celebrated book *Fear and Trembling*) loads up his son with the firewood, pretending that nothing unusual is about to happen. He acts as if they are headed toward a usual worship, and the son is granted the honor of carrying the wood. Abraham's confusing attitude toward Isaac is therefore one more pitiful attempt to repress—even if only for a few moments—the thought of the apparently unavoidable atrocity an to protect Isaac from the startling truth.

The reader's first impression of Abraham as an obstinate, hard-hearted, and cynical parent is misleading; behind that deceptive façade beats the heart of a merciful and desperate father. Yet, this initial baffling impression has its purpose. Abraham's deceitful command to his two young men, "abide ye here with the ass; and I and the lad will go yonder and worship, and come again to you" (v. 5), is no less perplexing.

Let me suggest the following justifications for Abraham's evasion. First, Abraham sought to protect Isaac, who was apparently present when Abraham spoke to his young men, from the horrible truth. Although he knew that this protection was temporary, Abraham's fatherly instinct spurred him to delay the disclosure of the truth.

Second, it was a humanistic concern and psychological instinct that led Abraham to also spare his young men the atrocious truth as long as possible.

Finally, there was another impulse that kept Abraham from verbalizing the dreadful event. Perhaps he wanted to believe that if he did not speak of the atrocity, there might be some possibility of avoiding it. One should be aware, in this context, of the psychological concepts of the ancient world that attributed great power to words, which served as a bridge between verbal expression and its materialization. Thus, Abraham's avoidance of expressing the truth was wishful thinking—a verbal articulation of the horrible truth might entail its execution. This is Abraham, the loving father.

However, Abraham, the pious believer, does not wish to tell the truth to the young servants, as he fears that once they know the true, horrid nature of God's command, they would stop Abraham and prevent him from fulfilling or obeying that command.

We may speculate as to which of the three options motivated Abraham's decision to conceal the truth, but there is a possibility that all three played an equal part. Although these potential justifications differ from each other, they share one common denominator: Abraham's great desire to repress the thought of the nightmarish future. Abraham's attempt to delay the atrocity gains more emphasis in light of the speed with which he (Abraham, the pious believer) follows God's instructions ("rose up early in the morning") when no time had been specified for the sacrifice. But again, we may conjecture that all three reasons for Abraham's reluctance to reveal the truth are equally valid, and the evasiveness of the author of these verses renders Abraham's character (the loving father vs. the pious believer) even more complex and intriguing.

In this respect, the rhetorical device, which makes the reader wonder about Abraham's perplexing acts (loading Isaac with burnt-offering wood; hiding the truth from his young men), has the same psychological function as the expressive presentation order: they both provide the reader with a peephole through which to view the biblical character's inner psychogenic mechanism, and they both deny the view that calls for an opaque and impenetrable psychological portrait of the biblical persona.

Abraham vs. Abraham

Another example of an intriguing rhetorical device enhancing psychological characterization can be found in the questionable role of the two young servants Abraham calls before leaving for the sacrifice. These young men are supposed to assist Abraham with the preparations for the trip.

Abraham's considerable wealth and high social status lead one to expect that his servants will carry out all necessary work. Thus, it is very surprising that Abraham does not let these servants perform their task, but prefers to do it himself. He is the one who saddles the asses and splits the wood for the burnt offering. By taking over his servants duties, Abraham, the loving father, aims to occupy himself with matters that will divert his thoughts from the frightful task at hand.

Indeed, Abraham's labor is much more demanding. Accordingly, he has to saddle at least six asses: one for himself, one for Isaac, two for the servants, and two to carry food, water, blankets, tents, and other materials for a long journey (six days in the desert).

Perhaps by engaging in his servants' duties, Abraham temporarily postpones the execution, and this delay offers another peek into Abraham's psychological make-up. Thus, Abraham's confusing behavior is nothing more than a rhetorical signpost calling the reader's attention to the character's psychological characterization. That and more. Abraham prefers to do all the physically demanding tasks by himself, while at the same time, slowing down the pace of the work to buy time and thus delaying the execution of his horrid mission.

Nevertheless, one may cogently argue that the "opposite" Abraham, the pious believer, refrains from asking his young servants to cleave the wood for the burnt offering (as well as saddling the asses), since he considers all those activities to be sacred and thus, no outsider should participate in them. Also, the fact that Abraham, the loving father, prefers to cleave the wood for the burnt offering by himself after already saddling the asses, even though he is physically exhausted, demonstrates his desperate wish to buy as much time as possible and delay carrying out his horrible mission.

It would seem that binding Isaac's chronicle to the altar of literary criticism can be quite rewarding: it brings to light not only the inner workings of the biblical text, its artistic and literary devices, but also its psychological motivations and underlying emotional currents.

In light of all the above, one may cogently argue that not one Abraham, but rather two considerably different Abrahams act in the story of the sacrifice (binding, *aqeda*) of Isaac: Abraham, the pious believer, who hastens to obey God's command despite its atrocious nature, and Abraham, the loving father, who does his very best to buy time, to postpone, to suspend God's horrid command.

When God appears to Abraham, He says to Abraham the following, "Take your son, your only son whom you love, Isaac" (Genesis 22;2). Indeed, ancient Talmudic scholars (about 2000 years ago) already suggested the following. The text displays a reciprocal dialogue between God and only God's voice is heard. The "cryptic," unheard voice of Abraham is overpowered and surrendered by God's voice. God says to Abraham, "Take your son."

Abraham vs. Abraham

And Abraham, the loving father, who is trying to buy time and postpone the execution of God's command, responds, "I have two sons."

God continues, "Your only son."

Abraham continues to pretend that he fails to understand God's command and says, "Each of my two sons is like my only son to me."

God does not give up, "... whom you love."

Abraham, still pretending his lack of understanding, replies, "I love both my sons equally."

At last, God runs out of patience and says almost reluctantly, "Isaac."

Undoubtedly, Abraham's seeming lack of comprehension surrenders the touching feelings of a loving father who is desperately trying to buy time and pretends that he does not understand God's atrocious command. It is also Abraham, the loving father, who refrains from instructing his two servants to prepare for the long journey into the desert and also preferring to do the exhausting labor of cleaving the wood for the burnt offering solely by himself. By doing both physically demanding tasks by himself, Abraham continues to buy time, hoping God may have a change of heart and take back His horrible command.

Yet one may equally argue that avoiding the work of the servants is a display of the opposite Abraham, the pious believer. Perhaps he considers the tiresome work of preparation for the long, arduous, physically demanding trek into the desert as sacred (for it complies with God's command), and thus he does not want anyone else to share that sacred activity.

Abraham lies to the servants (say that both he and Isaac will return after worshiping), as Abraham believes that as long as he does not verbalize the somber truth, that bleak, murky truth will not materialize.

Abraham, the pious believer, is introduced by lying to the servants, for he fears that once they learn about the atrocity he is about to commit, they will try to stop him and not allow him to fulfill God's command.

Hence, two different Abrahams are participants in the story of the sacrifice of Isaac: the loving father and the pious believer. The "conflict" between the two neither eclipses nor overshadows their fervent love of their son or the fervent love of their God.

A last observation. Isaac asks his father, Abraham, the following: "Here are the firestone and the wood, but where is the sheep for the burnt offering?" (Genesis 22;7) One object, however, Isaac fails to mention: *hama'chelet* (the knife). Is it possible that Isaac already suspects that he will be the one—and not the sheep—that will be slaughtered on the altar? The text does not surrender a hint that such a possibility might hold validity. Hence, it is up to the reader only to provide a plausible answer to that question. Filling in that gap of information is the biblical story's dexterous technique to ignite and propel the reader's innovative creativity.

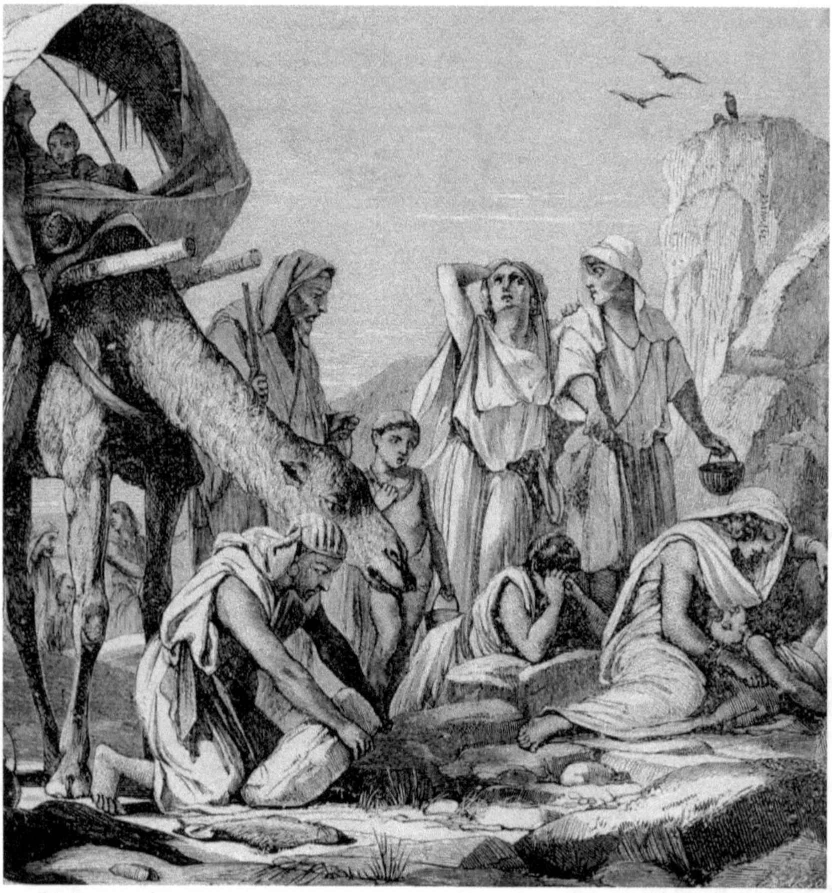

ABOUT ENIGMAS, ABOUT NAMING, AND ABOUT WOMEN IN THE BIBLE: A CLUSTER OF EXAMPLES

In Genesis 1; 26-27), one reads the following account of the creation of human beings: "And God said: Let us create man in our image (*tzalmenu*), after our likeness (*dmutenu*) ... And God created man in His image, in the image of God He created him..."

The first similarity between God and man (human being) is that while man should master all the beasts of the field, the birds of the sky, and the creeping creatures on the ground, God masters the entire universe. However, while God plans to create man in both His image and likeness, when He carries out His plan, the account says that He created man in his image (*tzalmo*) only, not in His likeness (*dmuto*).

What may be the reason for God's materializing only half of his initial plan? Why does God experience a change of heart? Perhaps God, in His divine knowledge, predicts the evil and wickedness that will be done by future human beings, and therefore, God does not wish to bestow upon human beings a full godly image any longer.

The full verse 27 is the following: "And God created man in His image. In the image of God, He created him; male and female, He created them."

It seems that God adds a new emendation to his original plan: not only creating man, but creating woman as well. Hence, the woman comes last; her creation follows that of man. It's as if God said to Himself, after planning to create man, "Just a minute. Let me add, at the very last moment, the creation of woman as well." Hence, from now on, the woman will always lag behind man, being considered secondary only.

Indeed, this is not true in all books and chronicles of the Bible. A book like Esther introduces the role of woman *vis à vis* man's differently. And there are other instances in the Bible in which women possess considerable power and influence, such as Dvorah (Deborah), Yael, Hulda, Samson's mother, Rebekah, and others. Nevertheless, the fact that woman was created last does foreshadow her inferiority throughout most of the books and events of the Bible. Thus, anti-feminism in the Bible is presented and practiced from the very beginning.

In Genesis 2; 5, one reads the following: "When the Lord God created earth and heaven, there were no shrubs of the field nor grasses of the field since God had not yet sent upon earth and there was no man to till the soil." It seems that the biblical text under consideration introduces two enigmatic contradictions.

First, after reading that no shrub had sprouted on earth since no rain had showered yet upon the earth, one reads the following; "A flow would well up from the earth and watered the entire face of earth." Thus, according to this verse, there is no reason to have rain, since earth was watered effectively by the flow (*ed*, in Hebrew, meaning vapor, flow). Hence, the text seems to contradict and

negate itself: the first declaration that no shrub had sprouted since God had not yet send rain on earth is invalid, does not hold water, since the vapor was perfectly sufficient to water the earth and make vegetation grow.

The second enigmatic contradiction is the following: while verse 26 argues that no vegetation had sprouted yet, since "there was no man to till the soil," one reads that God planted a garden, the Garden of Eden, where vegetation sprouted and thrived bountifully: "And from the earth, the Lord God caused to grow every tree that was delightful to the sight and good for eating, with the Tree of Life in the middle of the garden, and the Tree of Knowledge of Good and Evil" (verses 8-9).

Therefore, it seems that the initial argument that no shrub had sprouted yet because man was not yet there to till the soil is completely groundless. God does not need man's labor to create the most enticing garden.

In both cases, therefore, the biblical text seems to practice deconstruction: it challenges itself, it contests itself, it denies itself. Perhaps those two enigmatic contradictions derive from the fact that both contradictory texts stem from two different traditions or sources. One source is J (*Jehovah/Yahweh*) and the other source is E (*Elohim*). Hence, "the Lord" is J and God is E. However, from a literary viewpoint, perhaps this way, the biblical text introduces and offers two alternatives, two different kinds of interpretation. The biblical text seems to be generously liberal, providing the reader with two options while inviting the reader to choose one text that best agrees with the reader's credo.

Did the biblical writer plan the text to operate in such a complicated, even perplexing, fashion? It is hard to tell, probably even impossible. However, one thing is certain: an interpretation of a text of any sort should not try to unearth the latent intentions of the writer, but rather focus solely on the text itself. Only the text—rather than the assumed intention of the writer—is subject to textual investigation. The latter is perfectly sufficient, without "migrating" to turfs which are beyond the text *per se*.

In the flood story, God exterminated not only sinful mankind, but also the birds of the sky and the beasts of the field. "God (J) said, 'I will blot out from the earth the human beings which I created, men and women together with beasts of the field, all creeping creatures which creep on the ground and all birds of the sky, for I regret I created them' (Genesis 6; 7).

However, when God relates to malice and wickedness that ruthlessly prevail in the world, He mentions human beings only, and not creeping creatures, beasts of the field and birds of the sky: "God saw how grave was man's wickedness and how every plan devised by his mind was nothing but evil all the time" (Genesis 6;5).

Two questions seem to arise here: First, the fish of the sea do not share the same somber fate of human beings, beasts of the field, creeping creatures, and birds of the sky. The fish of the sea do not perish in the flood. Second, why should the birds and animals be exterminated when they are perfectly innocent?

Regarding the first question, it is nothing but a given that the waters of the flood will not exterminate the fish of the sea. After all, water is the nature habitat for fish. Regarding the animals and birds which will perish in the flood, the only explanation is that the wickedness in the world was so outrageous that it also afflicted the animals and birds.

That said, such an explanation does not seem persuasively valid. In what way can animals and birds commit iniquities? It is far from being clear, as animals and birds behave according to inherited instincts, while only human beings behave according to logical, emotional, and moral parameters. But what about infants, babies, and children? Are they also corrupt as adult human beings?

It thus seems that God Himself was afflicted by injustice. He does justice (exterminating evil human beings) while doing injustice (exterminating innocent animals, birds, babies, infants, and children). Ironically, God

Himself seems to be afflicted by the sins committed by human beings.

The latter statement brings to mind the destruction of the sinful cities of Sodom and Gemora (Genesis 19; 23-36). When God exterminates the wicked men and women of Sodom and Gemora, He simultaneously exterminates all vegetation, and even babies, infants, and children. In this case, too, God's actions are regretfully questionable.

In Genesis 21, one learns about the happy birth of Isaac, the son of old age, of Sarah and Abraham. Later, we read of Sarah's blatant demand that Ishmael be evicted after she saw him laughing (*metzachek*), stressing that "that son of a servant" will not share the inheritance with Isaac. Abraham is deeply distressed by that command, since Ishmael was his first-born son, his *bno*, as it is put in Hebrew. However, God instructs Abraham to obey Sarah's harsh command, promising that the youth would become the forefather of a great nation.

When Abraham sends Hagar and Ishmael into the wilderness early the next morning, he relates to Ishmael as "child" (*yeled*), despite the fact that Ishmael is at least fourteen years old. (He was thirteen when he was circumcised, a long time before he was evicted.) The word "child" relating to Ishmael keeps repeating (by his loving mother) when he is about to die of thirst in the wilderness. However, when God provides a well of fresh water and Ishmael is given water by his mother, Hagar ("that servant," as Sarah calls her with disdain and hatred), the angel of God calls Ishmael "youth" (*na'ar*) several times in accordance with his age.

The names of Ishmael (and also of Isaac) act here as apertures through which one can learn about the emotional attitude of the name-caller.

"Isaac" is "Itzchak" in Hebrew and means "laughter." In many biblical cases, laughter radiates sexual connotations, either positive or negative. In the case of Isaac/Itzchak, the sexual connotations are associated with fertility, with life. Indeed, Isaac continues the fertile lineage—life—of Abraham. When Ishmael laughs (*metzachek*), however, he displays sexual maturity that may eclipse the status of Isaac as the heir, since Ishmael is the first-born son of Abraham.

This is the reason Sarah calls Ishmael "the son of that servant," expressing both fear and hatred. When Abraham and Hagar call Ishmael "child" (*yeled*), they express much love and tenderness toward Ishmael.

When the angel of God relates to Ishmael, the angel calls him "youth" (*na'ar*) and expresses an objective perspective, one that relates to Ishmael by his actual age. Indeed, only once does God relate to Ishmael as "the son of the servant" (*ben ha'amah*), as Sarah does. However, in the case of God, He simply relates objectively to Ishmael, who was indeed the son of a servant.

Hence, each name acts in as a window through which emotions and mental attitudes of the name-callers are expressed.

Such is also the case in Genesis 12, the story of Abraham and Sarah descending into Egypt when famine ravaged the land of Canaan. (At this stage in the biblical texts, Abraham is still Abram and Sarah is still Sarai.)

Upon entry into Egypt, Abraham says to Sarah the following: "Please say that you are my sister, not my wife, and this way, I will benefit because of you and I will stay alive because of you." It is a matter of much interest that Abraham last mentions the most crucial reason, the one that will keep him alive, while first mentioning the "business" reason, the one that will benefit him with wealth. (This case was already addressed above.)

This way, the text piercingly scolds Abraham for putting his materialistic greed before the well-being of his wife. Indeed, he could have retreated and return to the land of Canaan and not let his wife be sold as a sexual object.

Abraham was a mighty, affluent leader of a tribe. He could have survived the famine in the land of Canaan. Nevertheless, Abraham chose to put priority on his economic well-being, without giving a second thought to the most disturbing fact that his wife, Sarah, would have to pay the price with her body and becoming the concubine of the king of Egypt (indeed wife).

Abraham's plot did materialize to the fullest: when he is showered with gifts from the king of Egypt, his very wording repeats: "And Abraham benefited because of her." In this way, the biblical narrator both ironically and blatantly rebukes Abraham. Abraham's unworthy attitude toward his wife is further enhanced by being portrayed as one who descended (*yarad*) to Egypt (a verb that yields derogatory connotations) and in this way, deserted the Promised Land, as one who descended to Egypt (*lagur*) to reside there. The only reason to add the verb "to reside" is to stress that Abraham deserted the Promised Land.

From the moment Abraham gives her to the Egyptians, his wife is no longer called Sarah, but "the woman" (*hayisha*). Thus, her new name reflects her new status as "sexual merchandise" and her personality is erased. That reflection enables the narrator to rebuke Abraham more blatantly for his greed.

* * * * *

When Rebekah gives birth to her twins, Jacob and Esau, one reads the following: "When her time to give birth was at hand, there were twins in her womb. The first one emerged red, like a hairy mantle all over, so they named him Esau. Then his brother emerged, holding to the heel of Esau, so they named him Jacob."

Here the names seem to reflect the nature and characteristics of the people who carry those names. Regarding Esau (*Esav*), it seems that this name is associated with the Hebrew verb *asah*, which means to do, to be active. Indeed, when Esau grew up, he was a very active man who also became a skillful hunter. In addition, he was the first one to emerge from his mother's womb, which also reflects energetic activity.

The case of the name Jacob (*Ya'akov* in Hebrew) is more complicated, since it reflects two contradictory characteristics. The name *Ya'akov* derives from the noun "heel," *akev* in Hebrew. Indeed, when Jacob/Ya'akov emerged from Rebekah's womb, he was holding onto Esau's heel. The latter does reflect plausibly Jacob's inclination to be a mellow man, one who retreats to the rear of the camp.

However, the name Ya'akov in Hebrew derives from the noun (also adjective) *akov*, which means something crooked, twisted, dishonest. Indeed, Jacob did deserve the second meaning of the name as well.

Jacob is the one who acts like a shrewd merchant when he buys the birthright from Esau for a bowl of lentil stew. And Jacob is the one who leads astray his old, blind father Isaac (while being goaded and motivated by his mother Rebekah) to steal Esau's birthright by getting the fatherly blessing from Isaac that rightfully belonged to Esau.

Jacob therefore deserves to the fullest the second, negative meaning of his name. (Also the first meaning, heel/*akev* is not particularly positive.) Even when Jacob became an old man, he did not prove to be better. When it came to his knowledge that his only daughter, Dinah, had been brutally raped and defiled, "he kept silent," (Genesis 34;5), being shamefully passive.

* * * * *

Also in the story of David and Bathsheba, naming reflects feelings and even scolding criticism (2 Samuel, Chapter 12). To gain Bathsheba, David put Uriah, her husband, to the sword of the Amonites, murdering Uriah both cunningly and brutally. The biblical narrator is furious with King David's murderous conduct.

One of the instruments the biblical narrator expresses his blatant rebuke of David is by naming Bathsheba in different ways. When Bathsheba learns that her husband Uriah the Hittite got killed in the battle, one reads the following: "When the wife of Uriah heard that her husband got killed, she lamented over her husband." The fact that the narrator calls Bathsheba "the wife of Uriah" instead of using her name, Bathsheba, with which the reader is already acquainted, stresses the fact that David initiated intimacy with her, and later killed her husband, while she was a married woman.

The same device, one which serves a moral purpose, is practiced again in the following verse: "God afflicted the child that Uriah's wife bore to David..." At that time, Bathsheba had already been David's wife for about eight months. Why, after having been David's wife for so long, after giving birth to David's son, does the narrator still refer to her as "Uriah's wife"? This way, the narrator continues scolding David for murdering Uriah, for taking Uriah's wife, and making her his own.

* * * * *

At the very vertex of the "*aqeda*" (binding) story, the story of the sacrifice of Isaac, one follows with great dread the

way the sacrifice is verbalized in a slow-motion fashion: "Abraham built an altar there; he laid out the wood; he bound his son Isaac; and Abraham picked up the knife to slaughter his son ..." (Genesis 22;9-10).

What is the reason for the tautology "his son Isaac"? After all, the reader already knows that Isaac is the name of Abraham's son. That tautology is not in vain: it stresses the horrendous fact that Abraham was commanded to slaughter his very beloved son.

In Hebrew, there are two words for a knife: *sakin*, which is commonly used in modern Hebrew, and *ma'achelet*, which is only used in biblical Hebrew. The word *ma'achelet* is the one used in the story of Isaac's sacrifice. That word is dramatically stronger than the word *sakin*, as *ma'achelet* radiates connotations of eating, of devouring. Hence, it is no wonder that that word was selected by the biblical narrator for this murderous story.

When Isaac asks his father, "Here are the fire-stone and the wood, but where is the lamb for the burnt offering?" he does not ask about a knife. Does this indicate that Isaac senses the atrocious role of the knife in the sacrifice ritual? It is hard to tell. (See previous discussion.)

What is certain, however, is that the naming of objects and people in the Bible is never random or arbitrary. The following case seems to echo that principle.

* * * * *

In the book of Exodus, when God appears to Moses for the very first time, commanding him to be the one who will lead to freedom the enslaved Israelites, God says to Moses the following: "I am the God of your father, the God of Abraham, the God of Isaac, and the God of Jacob."

One may question why God mentions Moses' father as one of the patriarchs of the Israelite nation. (God says *avicha*, which means "your father" and not *avotecha*, which means "your forefathers/ancestors.) Apparently, since God presents himself to Moses for the very first time, God wishes to enable Moses to better relate to that God. This way, relating to Moses' father, God makes Moses' mission more intimate, more understandable, more user-friendly.

* * * * *

As in all cases discussed above, wording and naming in the Bible are never in vain. They always carry meanings that should be deciphered by the reader. Once that latent meaning is revealed and deciphered, it is found to be very rewarding indeed.

The following last section of this chapter may be entitled, "The Importance of Being Verbal in the Bible" and aims to demonstrate the importance of verbal faculties in the Bible.

The Mishna sages already said, "*Ha'olam nivra bemilah*," the world was created by a word, relating to Genesis 1;3: "God said, let there be light and there was light."

Indeed, throughout the entire process of godly creation, the very same verbal formula keeps repeating: "God said let it be a firmament in the water" ... "God said let the water below the sky be gathered in one area" ... "God said let the waters bring forth swarms of living creatures" ...

"God said let the earth bring forth every kind of living creature" ...

If God wants to make clear to man that he cannot have an animal spouse, He makes man a verbal creator: man gives names to animals of all kinds and this way, he "verbally creates" them. Thus, God also makes man realize that he is superior to the animals and cannot choose one of them to be his spouse. (Some of the following cases were already discussed above.)

The opposite case is demonstrated with man's naming of his spouse, "woman" (*Isha*), since she came out of man (*Ish*). This way, man ensures his superiority over the woman: he names her, he "verbally creates" her.

After creating the woman verbally, man verbalizes his creation in the form of a poem:

> This one at last
> Is bone of my bones
> And flesh of my flesh.
> This one shall be called woman
> For from man she was taken.

This poem, verbalized by man, further displays his verbal faculties, which enable him to act as a "verbal creator."

When the biblical narrator wishes to belittle woman's intellectual faculties (she breaches God's command and eats the forbidden fruit only because she wishes to acquire knowledge), He makes her stumble on verbal grounds. Accordingly, He causes her to confuse the names of the two prominent trees in the Garden of Eden. While she has in mind the Tree of Knowledge of Good and Evil, she says

the name of the Tree in the Middle of the Garden, which is the "surname" of the Tree of Life.

Verbal faculties condition intellectual faculties. There is no way to address an issue intellectually without possessing the capacity to verbalize it. Hence, belittling woman as an intellectual person is materialized by belittling her verbal faculties, as is demonstrated by her verbally confusing the names of the two trees.

In the case of the city of Babel and its tall tower, verbalization is equally demonstrated. God decides to destroy the erected tower, which aimed to pierce the sky, as He considered its construction an act of intolerable haughtiness. The way God materializes His decision is by confounding the language of the people who erected that arrogant tower. Deprived of their verbal capacity, the people fail to communicate with one another and can no longer continue the arrogant tower's construction. In this case, deprivation of verbal faculties yields an existential incapability.

It is a matter of interest that only after construction of the tower ceases, the city earns its name Babel (from the Hebrew root *b.l.l.*, to confound, to confuse). What is the point of naming a city after it ceases to exist? This way, the city turns into a symbol that warns people not to practice hubris.

After God appears to Abraham for the very first time, making him realize that he is God's chosen prophet, Abraham builds an altar dedicated to God, who appeared to him. Almost at the very same time Abraham builds a second alter to God, at which he invoked God by name. What is the reason for the second altar?

The second time the altar is built while invoking God by name. The latter demonstrates an intellectual aware-ness that is materialized through words. Thus, in the second altar dedicated to God, Abraham plausibly displays a more profound and more elevated acquaintance with God.

God also changes Abram's name into Abraham (meaning "elevated father") and Sarai's name to Sarah (meaning "ruler"). This act of verbalization reflects the elevation of both Abraham and Sarah in God's grand plan. That and more. By renaming Abram (Abraham) and Sarai

(Sarah), both of them earn the Hebrew letter *heh* (h in English transliteration), which stands for God in Hebrew.

God commands Abraham to name his future son Itzchak, which is entomologically associated with laughter. As previously discussed in this chapter, laughter in the Bible may be associated with sexual connotations, either positive or negative. In the case of the name of Itzhak, the sexual connotations are absolutely positive, since they mean fertility, life.

Thus, verbalization in the Bible is engaged with various meanings that serve the biblical narrator in delivering his message. The latter may be ideological, historical, religious, moral, national, social, or other. However, the biblical text does always deliver a message in the hope that it will be correctly deciphered by the text's target audience.

When a Horizontal Sequence Meets its Redemption

One of the most notable phenomena of the literary text is a paratactic order of presentation. In this phenomenon, the textual sequence consists of a list of objects/words/verbs that are almost identical, or at least very similar. This sequence is horizontal, since it possesses no internal mechanism that can extricate it from its cumulative, unfolding momentum. Thus, there is a need for an extricating mechanism to lead the text to its termination.

Such a mechanism is usually a new element (object/word/verb), entirely alien to the elements in the paratactic sequence. Such a different element (like *Deus ex machina*), which forces itself upon the sequential text, leads the paratactic sequence toward its termination.

A persuasive example for the latter is to be found in Genesis 12. After God blesses Abram/Abraham, one reads the following:

"Abram WENT forth as God had commanded him and Lot WENT with him. Abram was seventy-five years of age when he LEFT Haran. Abram TOOK his wife Sarai and his brother's son Lot and all the wealth which they had AMASSED and all the persons which they PURCHASED in Haran, and they SET OUT for the land of Canaan. When they ARRIVED in the land of Canaan, Abram PASSED through the land as far as the site of Shechem, at the oaks of Mamreh and the Canaanites are settled in the land."

Here, the paratactic order of presentation in this brief paragraph consists of a list of very active verbs: went, went, left, took, amassed, purchased, set out, arrived, passed. Only the very last verb in this list—*are settled*—is passive. This is indeed the literary mechanism that "forces" itself on the text, extricates it from the horizontal, paratactic sequence, and leads it to an end.

The fact that the extricating verb is so different from the many previous verbs emphasizes the "message" of this verb: the Canaanites are already rooted in the Promised Land. This way, the text stresses that in order to earn the Promised Land, Abram will have to fight forcefully.

Until then, the impression was that Abram would get the Promised Land on a silver platter. Hence, the fact that Abram will have to encounter mounds of life-threatening challenges before and upon getting to the Promised Land is deftly emphasized by the extricating mechanism that leads the paratactic sequential text to its end.

A similar example is introduced by the end of the story in which Esau sells his birthright to his twin brother Jacob for a bowl of lentil stew. It is a matter of much interest how the two brothers reverse their roles. Esau, the powerful hunter, becomes exceedingly weak, almost to the point of death, when he is hungry. And Jacob, initially described as a mellow, shy, passive man, acts like a cunning merchant—he forces his brother to vow (today!) that he will sell him his birthright for some food. (Mind the usage of the verb "to sell" in this context, one that stressed the unexpected portrayal of Jacob as a shrewd merchant.)

The deal is done. Hungry Esau gets his bowl of lentil stew after he makes an oath that Jacob forces him to take. As a shrewd, cunning merchant, Jacob insists that Esau will vow *today*!

The story ends with the following verbs: "[Esau] ate, drank, rose, left, and spurned/despised his birthright." This sequential list of active verbs operates like a paratactic order of presentation. Indeed, the very last verb—*"spurned/despised the birthright"*—is very different, as it reflects a *passive* act of surrender.

This very last passive verb, which is considerably different from the previous active ones, acts in the capacity of an extricating mechanism that leads the paratactic sequence to its end. Also in this case, the operation of the extricating mechanism carries its most significant meaning. Both brothers prove to be unworthy: Jacob, who takes advantage of his brother's physical distress, and Esau, who so easily sells his birthright for a bowl of lentil stew.

Hence, in both cases discussed, the horizontal, paratactic sequence is dexterously severed and meets its "redemption" while delivering a meaningful message.

A Man for No Season: Samson in the Cage of His Childishness

The following discussion focuses on the character and chronicles of the last judge, Samson. Since one of the prominent points of this discussion is associated with comic characteristics, it will be useful to start the discussion with some theoretical observations concerning the nature of the comic mechanism, notably the way it is portrayed and analyzed by Henri Bergson in his celebrated book, *Le Rire* (Laughter).

Bergson argues that laughter can take place only in the realm of human beings and not in the realms of animals or non-living objects. Laughter can stem, however, from "installing" in a human being a mechanic repetition, such as a clown in the circus who falls down and gets up repeatedly. Hence, laughter derives from the repetition of the same action by a human being who operates like a machine.

Already in this early stage of the discussion, one may trace many repetitions in the behavior and actions of Samson: he is attracted to foreign/Philistine women only; he keeps repeating the same mistakes; he repeatedly launches devastating raids in the Philistine territory, which receive a brutal response from the Philistines; he is repeatedly betrayed by the Philistine women; and he is repeatedly connected with the fire motif (including the fact that his name [*Shimshon*] derives from the word "sun" [*shesh*] in Hebrew). To laugh, one must create a distance between himself/herself and the subject of the laughter.

The fact that Samson acts by himself only and fails to fulfill the divine prophecy that he will start redeeming the Israelites from the oppressive yoke of the Philistines, "isolates" Samson in his lonely realm and his childish narcissism, and creates a distance between him and the reader. That distance enables the comic mechanism to operate.

Both Bergson and Freud argue that laughter only has social characteristics and is devoid of psychological characteristics. Following that vein, both Bergson and

Freud consider laughter a tool that enables the reader/ spectator to view himself/herself in a social context, which is social decorum.

I respectfully take issue with both Bergson and Freud. I believe that laughter is engaged with the reader's/ spectator's psychological mechanism. We laugh when we witness a repetition of the same action. By our human nature, we love the repetitious momentum because it confers upon us a feeling of stability, security, tranquility, and serenity. In this way, for instance, an infant enjoys being lulled by his mother and an adult enjoys the momentous movement while practicing physical intimacy.

Although these two examples are not associated with laughter, they resemble, for instance, the momentous movements of the clown in a circus who keeps falling down and getting up, causing the audience to react with laughter. Laughter is a physiological manifestation of the audience's pleasure (which is psychologically oriented), while experiencing and enjoying the momentous movement and its repetition.

For that very reason, human beings do not appreciate surprises, as these violate the momentous movement that conceives a sense of stability, security, and serenity. In fact, we, as human beings, do not like surprises. They upset the certainty and tranquil stability of the momentous repetitions by breaching and frustrating expectations. In this context, one may ask the following: if human beings do not like surprises that upset and deny the serenity of their expectations, why do we laugh when we hear a joke that consists entirely of frustrated expectations?

In this case, the laughter is a physiological expression, one that is associated with relief: whatever happens in the surprising joke happens to somebody else, not to us. Hence we are redeemed of the unpleasant "destiny" of the one who is the subject of our laughter; we are "off the hook."

According to Bergson, the most typical characteristic of the comic character is hubris, or haughtiness. The latter can be easily identified with Samson: he acts alone, singlehandedly, without listening to any advice (his parents advise him to refrain from marrying a Philistine woman) while believing that nobody knows better than he does. Being so sure that his physical strength can extricate him from any trouble, he does not pay attention to the most tangible threat of the Philistines. He fails to realize that his own nation is distressed due to his brutal raids, which are sometimes murderous. He acts as if the entire world has been placed in the palm of his hand, and he can squeeze it and crush it at his convenience.

There is no historical or archaeological evidence that Samson ever existed. He is engaged in the Bible with the period of the judges (he was the last judge), 1200 BCE–1000 BCE, which was the period of the conquest of some parts of the land of Canaan. (According to some modern biblical archeologists and historians, the early Israelis did not come from the outside, as they branched from local Canaanites, and conquered only relatively small territories in the land of Canaan.) Undoubtedly, Samson was very different from all Israelite judges and leaders.

Before he was born to his barren mother, she was told by the angel of God that he would be a Nazarite whose hair

would never be touched and he would start redeeming his nation from the oppressive yoke of the Philistines (Judges 13;5). The fact that he would only start to redeem his nation and would not bring full redemption foreshadows the fact that eventually Samson would be very far from bestowing upon his nation any redemption whatsoever.

On the contrary, his constant raids against the Philistines, which stemmed from his private feelings of rage and revenge, caused much aggravation to the Israelites. The devastating outcome of those raids goaded the Philistines into severely punishing the Israelites.

The circumstances of Samson's birth to his barren mother (her name is not mentioned) brings to mind barren Sarah, who gave birth to Isaac; barren Hana, who bore the prophet Samuel; barren Rachel, who gave birth to Joseph and Benjamin; and barren Rebekah, who gave birth to Esau and Jacob.

The circumstances of the birth of Samson, following celestial intervention, are deftly discussed by David Grossman in his worthy book, *Lions' Honey: The Story of Samson*. Like other barren women in the Bible who eventually give birth to excellent sons (Sarah, Hana, Rachel, Rebekah), the barren mother of Samson eventually gives birth.

The beginning of the chronicles of Samson, and notably the circumstances of his birth, are a foreshadowing introduction that augurs the rest of the story: dominant women who trap Samson and a weak male protagonist (Samson) who, despite his extraordinary physical strength, is weak in comparison to the women in his life (his first Philistine wife and later, the Philistine Delilah), as well as the Philistine harlot, who probably notified the Philistine men who sought to kill Samson, that Samson would be with her in the town of Gaza.

Twice the angel of God appeared to the barren mother of Samson. However, when the mother reports the unusual event to her husband, she does not use the verb "to appear." Instead, she utilizes the verb "to come," which is associated in the Bible with sexual intercourse. For instance, Abraham "came" to Hagar and she conceived (Genesis 16;4).

The husband, however, prays to God while asking Him to send the angel again so he will guide them in raising the exceptional son to be born. The angel is sent again to fulfill his mission. Despite the fact that the husband wished to encounter the angel, the angel prefers to come again to the mother while she is alone in the field. The text stresses that her husband is not with her and uses the verb "to come" to portray the erotic encounter between the angel and the mother. (Early biblical commentators already noted the meaningful sexual connotations associated with the biblical verb *lavoh*, "to come," while raising the possibility that there was a sexual encounter between Samson's mother and the divine harbinger.)

Alluding twice to a possible sexual encounter between the mother and the angel further emphasizes the weakness and passiveness of the husband. The latter earns further validity, as the name of the husband is Manoach, a name that is etymologically engaged with passiveness. Indeed, in modern Hebrew, the word *manoach* means a dead man, the very embodiment of passiveness.

Furthermore, when the mother shares with her husband the good tidings about the exceptional son who is going to be born, she does not tell her husband the national mission of the son—to start redeeming Israel from the oppressive yoke of the Philistines.

That omission is neither random nor arbitrary. It demonstrates the fact that the passive husband is not "worthy" of being notified of the national mission of the son. Hence the husband who is left behind portends Samson who will also be "left behind" by the shrewdness of his two Philistine women, his first wife and Delilah.

Addressing this "prophecy" from another angle, one may plausibly argue that the father, Manoach, is "betrayed" by his wife (twice in the allusions to sexual encounters between the angel and the mother, and again when she fails to tell him about Samson's national mission) in the same way as Samson is betrayed by his first wife, who coaxes Samson to surrender the meaning of his riddle, and by Delilah, who surrenders his secret of might to the Philistines.

The passiveness and weakness of the father foretell Samson's fate: he is expected only to *start* redeeming Israel without completing his mission. Eventually, however, the reader realizes that Samson will fail even to start redeeming Israel from the oppressive yoke of the Philistines. Instead of starting to save his tormented nation, he confers upon it distress.

It is a matter of much interest that fire plays a prominent role in the chronicles of Samson. For example, his name (*Shimshon*) derives from the noun "sun" (*shemesh*) in Hebrew. When his father and mother sacrifice a burnt offering to God, we read about the flame that ascends high above, and later the angel is seen in the flame (Judges 13;20).

In the wedding feast of Samson and his Philistine wife, the Philistines who participate in the feast threaten the bride by telling her that if she will not tell them the meaning of Samson's riddle "they shall put her and her father's household to fire" (ibid., 14;15). When Samson finds out that his wife was given to another man, he takes revenge on the Philistines in the following fashion: "Samson went and caught three hundred foxes. He took torches, and turning the foxes tail to tail, he placed a torch between each pair of tails. He lit the torches and turned the foxes loose among the standing grain of the Philistines, setting fire to stacked grain, vineyards, and olive groves" (ibid., 15;4-5).

When Samson is arrested and bound with ropes by 3,000 men of Judah who wished to give him to the Philistines, "The spirit of God gripped him, and the ropes on his arms became like flax that catches fire" (ibid., 15;14). When Delilah binds him, "he pulled the tendons apart, as a strand of straw comes apart at the touch of fire" (ibid., 16;9).

The motif of fire in the chronicles of Samson is meaningful: like Samson, fire is both powerful and destructive. In this respect, the motif of fire metaphorically reflects Samson's most distinguished characteristics.

After Samson was born and became a young man, the text notes: "The spirit of God first moved (inspired) him in the encampment of Dan, between Zorah and Eshtaol" (ibid., 13;25). On the one hand, the fact that the spirit of God was upon Samson most certainly carries positive connotations. On the other hand, however, the fact that the celestial inspiration with which Samson was endowed was limited to such a small place (walking distance from end to end) is metaphorically ironical, as it reflects the fact that he was expected to start redeeming

Israel, but nothing beyond that (bringing full redemption to his people).

Childishness is one of Samson's most prominent characteristics. After he tore the lion asunder with his bare hands, he says nothing to his parents (ibid., 14;6). The reason for this enigmatic behavior is that like a child, he is not aware of his own strength, and correspondingly, slaying a lion with his bare hands is considered by Samson a matter of daily routine that is not associated with anything exceptional.

The way Samson feeds his parents with honey, also using his bare hands, brings to mind a child who relates to his parents on an infantile level. When Delilah "lulls him to sleep on her lap" (ibid., 16;19), Samson is like an infant. Indeed, more than once he sleeps like a child in the presence of Delilah.

Describing Samson as a child brings to mind the comic aspect in his image. On the one hand, he was chosen by God even before he was born. On the other hand, however, he is portrayed like a child. That discrepancy between the expectations and their frustration creates a gulf that is like a joke, a source of a comic relief.

Samson acts like a child while being motivated by impulses and emotionalism. The latter is reflected even in his riddle, which is entirely devoid of any rational, intellectual inclinations as it consists of one personal occurrence that happened to Samson, slaying the lion with his bare hands, which cannot be deciphered in any logical way whatsoever.

As already mentioned, the repetitions in the acts of Samson (his attraction to Philistine women who betray

him; the vengeance raids he launches against the Philistines); his repeatedly occurring depictions of him sleeping
like a child, bring to mind a mechanism that is installed in
a human body and acts like a *perpetuum mobile*. The
motional repetitions, as well as the denied expectations
(one expects a human being to act like a human being and
not like a machine) produce a comic effect. In this respect
Samson operates like a comic hero.

On the other hand, however, Samson is also associated with a tragic hero, an individual who is more elevated than mediocre society and is expected to free society from a state of calamity. (See the case of ancient Greek tragedy.) Such a description fits Samson who fails to remedy society (his nation) even partially. The end of Samson (who, like a tragic hero, is doomed to be evicted from society when his mission is completed) does possess a magnificent tragic echo: "Samson cried 'Let me die with the Philistines' and he pulled [the temple's pillars] with all his might. The temple came crashing down all the lords and all the people in it. Those who were slain by him as he died outnumbered those who had been slain by him when he lived" (ibid., 16;30). The fact that the comic aspects associated with Samson are wrapped by tragic issues creates an aesthetic balance that confers captivating intricacy on the chronicles of Samson.

JOSEPH WHO?
UNMASKING THE REAL JOSEPH

Biblical Joseph was the son of old age of Jacob, who Rachel, Jacob's more beloved wife, bore to him (later she died giving birth to the twelfth son of Jacob, Benjamin). Jacob loved Joseph, his son of old age, much more than he loved his other sons (Genesis 37). As a demonstration of his special love for Joseph, Jacob made for him a "*ktonet passim,*" which is wrongly translated as "a coat of many colors," or "ornamented tunic," while its literal translation is a "striped tunic."

There is neither historical nor archeological evidence that supports the theory that Joseph ever existed. The Egyptians were very meticulous about documenting their historical and social chronicles. Hence, it is rather peculiar that a dramatic figure like Joseph, a foreigner who becomes the master of the land of Egypt, who redeems and rescues Egypt from the most oppressive famine, is not mentioned at all in the countless Egyptian documents.

The only possibility that Joseph did exist as an historical figure is that he ruled (next to Pharaoh) the land of Egypt during the period of the Hyksos, a Semitic nation that invaded Egypt in the 17th through the 16th centuries BCE. The Hyksos did not leave much documentation and it may be likely that being Semitic, they would tolerate the powerful role of another Semite, the foreigner Joseph, in the land of Egypt. The word "Hyksos" means "rulers of foreign countries." That and more. It is said that the Egyptians disdained shepherds. Joseph was a shepherd, thus only the Hyksos would tolerate and embrace him.

As a biblical character, however, Joseph had attracted —indeed, to this very day—much attention and admiration. The sages of the Hebrew *Mishna* called him Joseph the Righteous. They considered him entirely flawless. As the biblical narrative unfolds, Joseph, as a 17-year-old lad, had dreams of blatant hubris and haughtiness. "Once Joseph and a dream which he told to his brothers; and they hated him even more. He said to them, 'Hear this dream which I have dreamed. There we were binding sheaves in the field, when suddenly my sheaf stood up and remained upright; then your sheaves gathered around and bowed low to my sheaf.'"

His brothers answered, "Do you mean to reign over us? And they hated him even more for his talk about this dreams. He dreamed again (according to his testimony) and told it to his brothers, saying, "Look, I have had another dream, and this time the sun, the moon, and eleven stars were bowing down to me."

And when he told it to his father and his brothers, his father berated him. "What," he said to him, "is this dream you have dreamed? Are we to come, I and your mother and your brothers and bow low to you to the ground?" So his brothers were wrought up at him, and his father kept the matter in mind." (Genesis 37; 5-11).

Hence, one must be immensely haughty to dream such dreams and equally insensitive to tell those dreams to the ones who are blatantly humiliated in those dreams. The level of arrogance and audacity displayed by Joseph is undisputed. In return, the brothers conspired to kill him when he visited them in their pasturing place. However, both Reuben and Judah contest that murderous plot and the brothers sold Joseph to a caravan of Ishmaelites (also named Midianites) that was heading for Egypt.

In Egypt, Joseph was bought as a slave by Potiphar, the courtier and chief steward of Pharaoh. Until this point (and later on, as will be later discussed), Joseph fails to demonstrate even a sliver of righteousness. He is haughty, arrogant, insensitive, and the fact that he was sold as a slave does not make him righteous. Indeed, his uncontrolled haughtiness was the reason for being sold as a slave. This does not mean that the punishment for arrogance should be being sold as a slave. Nevertheless, the latter is far from making him righteous.

The sages of the *Mishna* did not only consider him a righteous person, but also stressed that he was a person who prudently and morally tamed his instincts, such as sexual lust. On top of that, in Hassidism, Joseph is a symbol of sacredness and laudable capacity to say no to a sin. Apparently, the latter relates to the idle attempt of Photiphar's wife to sexually tempt Joseph and he resisted.

Indeed, after Potiphar made him the master of his house and treated him with both generosity and respect, perhaps even admiration, resisting the temptation of that lustful woman was the most practical reaction upon the part of Joseph. He did realize to the fullest what he could lose had he surrendered to Potiphar's wife.

Correspondingly, Joseph was not a righteous person who admirably tamed his sexual instincts, but rather, a well-calculated young man who did not want to risk losing his entire world for having sex with his master's wife. Later on, after Joseph deciphers wisely the two agitating dreams of Pharaoh (the motif of dreams keeps repeating through the chronicles of Joseph, while turning into a catalyst that shapes his destiny), he becomes the master of the entire land of Egypt, during both the period of abundance and the period of famine which he foretold while unearthing the latent meaning of Pharaoh's dreams. Accordingly, Pharaoh appointed Joseph to be the master of Egypt.

The famine also hit the land of Canaan and Jacob sent his ten sons to procure rations in the land of Egypt, where Joseph had gathered reserve grain during the seven years

of bountiful abundance for the following seven years of blatantly biting famine. When the brothers saw Joseph, they failed to recognize him. He recognized them but pretended that they were strangers to him. When they faced him, they bowed down to the ground: Joseph's dreams turned truthful. However, he treated them harshly, accusing them of being spies who came to unveil "the nakedness of the land" (while they had left him naked in the pit in the desert before he was sold to the Ishmaelites). Ironically, Joseph had previously acted as a spy while tarnishing his brothers behind their backs.

From then on, the entire plot of the story focuses on the vicious ways in which Joseph treats his brothers, leads them astray, frightens them, and humiliates them. Indeed, the brothers were not a group of saints and they did deserve to be punished. However, Joseph proved to be a master of taking revenge on those who deserved it.

The sages of the *Mishna* stress that the righteousness of Joseph is also displayed in his laudable ability not to carry a grudge and take revenge. Joseph is the last one who can be portrayed in such a fashion. Indeed, when Joseph eventually makes himself known to his brothers and quits harassing and intimidating them, he kisses and cries on each one's shoulder. They, however, seem to restrain their feelings and show no affection toward Joseph. They cannot easily forget the malicious way in which he treated them. In Leviticus 19;18, one reads the following: "You shall not take vengeance or bear a grudge." Indeed, Joseph does both and most blatantly indeed.

Joseph the Righteous, who controls his instincts, who takes no revenge? Not in my Bible.

Joseph, being oblivious to the feelings of others (Jacob his father, his brothers, as Joseph practically forces them to hear his dreams of extreme haughtiness) is displayed in the following fashion. When Joseph recognizes his brothers, he recalls his dreams and correspondingly, he speaks to them harshly. It is as if his dreams were perfectly fine and thus justified his harsh attitude toward his brothers. Again, Joseph's arrogance prevents him from being sensitive to the distress of others.

One more element proves how wrong it is to call Joseph "righteous." From the voyages of his brothers to Egypt and back to the land of Canaan, it seems that such a voyage was quite customary and not complicated by too many challenges or stumbling blocks. Hence, if the brothers could rather easily go on such voyages, for Joseph, the lord of the entire land of Egypt, one who is second only to the Pharaoh, such a relatively short and reasonably comfortable voyage could easily be completed by Joseph. However, Joseph apparently is not very interested in seeing his father Jacob in the land of Canaan.

The latter attitude is reflected in the name Joseph gives his first-born son, Menasheh. This name derives from the biblical root *n.s.h.*, which means to forget, to forsake. Joseph explains the reason he named his first-born son Menasheh: "God has made me forget completely my hardship and my parental home." The latter statement further stresses the fact that Joseph behaved like an indifferent son who is not interested in finding out how his father—the one who loved him so deeply—was doing. No recollections, no caring, no wishing to pay his respects to his lamenting, heartbroken, old father, no emotional attachment—nothing. This portrays Joseph as a indifferent, ungrateful son, who is willing to forget his loving, old father. Not even a postcard during those many years.

Joseph the Righteous? Not the person who is entirely oblivious, entirely indifferent when it comes to the well-being of his very loving father, who could not be comforted once he believed Joseph was gone forever; the very same Joseph who takes bitter revenge out on his dismayed brothers.

Joseph the Righteous? Forget about it. Indeed, Joseph himself forgot about it. Joseph, the spoiled son and brother, compels his brothers and father to listen to his haughty dreams, in which his father and brothers bow down before him, and in this way, are humiliated. Indeed, that part of the dreams did materialize in Egypt, when the brothers are harshly investigated by Joseph. Nevertheless, only a person who is shamefully devoid of common sense, of being oblivious to the feelings of others, can loudly declare such dreams.

The text continues to announce that Joseph is far from being righteous. Joseph the Righteous? As previously stated, there is no such man, at least not in my Bible.

CHERCHEZ LA FEMME, OR WHOSE TRAGEDY IS THIS ONE? THE SCROLL OF ESTHER

It seems impossible (for the time being at least) to trace a plausibly solid historical background to the chronicles that are unfolded in the Scroll of Esther. Many scholars argue that the king Achasveros is indeed the Persian king Chashairish (Xerex in Greek), who reigned for twenty years in the fifth century BCE (485 BCE–465 BCE). He reached the throne at the age of thirty-five and was the fourth generation after the founder of the Persian dynasty, King Cyrus.

King Chashairish earned fame due to the luxurious feasts he initiated, the numerous precious presents he endowed, and the many women he loved. In this respect, King Achasveros in the Scroll of Esther fits the historical image of the Persian king. King Chashairish was also known for his brutal response to the rebellion of the Babylonians and his many wars against Egypt.

It is a matter of much interest that in archaeological digging in the ancient Sumerian city Borsphia a reference to a treasury clerk was found. The name of that treasury clerk is Marduka. The resemblance of that name to the name "Mordechai" (Esther's uncle, who adopted and raised her) in the Scroll of Esther is compelling. Apparently, both names stem from the name Marduk, the most elevated god in the mythological Babylonian pantheon.

Scholars assume that the Scroll of Esther was composed in the fourth century BCE, not later than 330 BCE, the year in which Persian rule was severed due to the conquest of Alexander the Great. It is quite apparent that the writer of the Scroll of Esther was well acquainted with the Persian language, as well as the capital city Shusha/Shushan.

The fact that the Scroll of Esther includes no Greek cultural elements verifies the assumption that it was composed in the fourth century BCE, prior to the spread of Greek culture. Many scholars argue that the Scroll of Esther echoes the ancient Babylonian myth that focuses on the return and thriving of the spring. Indeed, that ancient myth derives from a more ancient source: the period that the Assyrian and Accadian empires were united and their highly developed culture produced intricate mythology (2371 BCE–2316 BCE). Such a myth was cultivated later by the ancient Greeks, who believed in the death of the fertility god in winter and its resurrection in spring. Indeed, the cycle of death in winter, followed by the resurrection in spring, is echoed by ancient, classical Greek tragedies and even by some modern Western tragedies.

It seems quite likely that Mordechai reflects the god Marduk and Esther reflects Ishtar, the ancient Babylonian goddess of fertility (see in the Hebrew Bible Ashtoret, who is associated with the tree Ashera). In the Babylonian

myth, Marduk and Ishtar are cousins, and similar is the case with Mordechai and Esther.

In the Babylonian myth, Marduk and Ishtar struggled with two ancient gods of Eilam mythology and came out victorious. These gods are Human (the Glorious One) and Mashti (the Beautiful One), and it is quite feasible that they are represented in the Scroll of Esther by Haman and Vashti (who earned acclaim due to her beauty).

In addition, the feminine name *Hadashtu* (a new bride) from Accadian mythology corresponds to the second name of Esther, Hdassah, who was also a new bride.

The Scroll of Esther is the only book among the other books compiled in the Hebrew Bible in which the name of

God is not mentioned even once (even in Song of Songs, which is so secular and erotic by nature, there is a reference to the name of God, *shalhevetyah*, "the flame of God"). Indeed, the Scroll of Esther is the only biblical book that was not found among the Dead Sea Scrolls, which include all the books of the Bible (only the book of Isaiah in a complete form).

Sages of the Talmud, however, argue that the phrase "rescue and redemption will reach the Jews from another source" is an indirect reference to God (Esther 4:14).The fact, however, that the Septuagint and the Vulgate bibles include prayers to God recited by Mordechai and Esther is evidence that later biblical scholars did not feel comfortable with the fact that the name of God is not mentioned in the Scroll of Esther.

Chapter 1 opens with the spectacular feast that Achasveros conducts, one that takes many days. His wife, Vashti, also conducts a feast for the women. When the king's heart finds favor in the wine, he commands that Queen Vashti appears at his feast to display her beauty. Queen Vashti, however, surprises both the king and the reader by refusing to meet the king's command, a rebellious action unheard of in the vast kingdom.

From a structuralist-rhetorical perspective, one may discern here a foreshadowing hint that another rebellion aimed at the king will surface later in the unfolding plot. It is unclear why Queen Vashti engages in a refusal that may lead to her execution. Nevertheless, her refusal to obey the king's command does manifest a courageous, "feminist," assertive act.

Whether Vashti was evicted from the royal court or was executed is not clear. What is clear, however, is that the furious king is found out as a weak, senseless character who is entirely dependent on his shrewd advisors' direction. The king is advised to send a decree to all 127 nations under his rule. That decree commands all wives to respect and obey their husbands and disregard the "unworthy" example set by Queen Vashti.

Chapter 2 starts with a rhetorical device that consists of cultivating expectations and frustrating expectations. At the very beginning of the chapter, one reads the following: "After these matters passed, the king's fury calmed down and he recalled Vashti." One is at liberty to cultivate positive expectations that once the king's rage faded away, he was willing to forgive his rebellious wife. Nevertheless, these expectations are denied and breached in no time. Accordingly, after the king recalls his wife, he is advised by his cunning advisors to bring to the capital city of Shushan, "hosts" of good-looking, young female virgins and select one of them to be the new queen.

Suddenly, however, that new track of the plot is interrupted by unveiling expositional material that does not belong to the course of the plot. By its nature, this expositional material (like any such material) is aesthetically problematic. It belongs to the past of the plot and for that reason, suffers from two flaws: it is not as relevant to the current focus of interest and attraction, and it happened before the plot started, and therefore, is passive compared to the appealingly active plot. Thus the work of literature's implied author suspends the expositional material until the reader encounters in the plot a gap that he/she fails to fill without gaining that expositional material.

The expositional material is released to the reader only when it is urgently required to fill the gap and to intelligently follow the unfolding occurrences of the plot. This

way, the expositional material earns aesthetic attractive-
ness, one which it lacks due to its two aesthetic flaws.
Hence, in the midst of the evolvement of the plot in chapter 2, unexpected expositional material is inserted, which
focuses on Mordechai and his step-daughter/niece Esther.
The text that follows, however, unveils the reason for
interlacing that expositional material to the plot.

Because of Esther's exceptional beauty and charm, she
is also taken to the royal court as a candidate for the
future wife of the king.

The chapter ends with one more section of pseudo-
expositional text that seems to upset the fluent evolution
of the plot. That pseudo-expositional material shares with
the reader how Mordechai heard about an attempt to
launch a rebellion and kill the king. Mordechai shared that
information with Esther and she told the king. The matter
was investigated and the two officers of the royal court
who plotted the rebellion were executed.

Unexpectedly, Mordechai does not gain any recognition
or favor for saving the king's life. The latter opens a gap
that will be filled out later, when its timing "ripens." In the
meantime, however, one more gap opens. Instead of
learning whether (and when) Mordechai will be handsomely rewarded for saving the king's life, the reader discovers
how Haman earns the king's unlimited confidence and
becomes the most powerful and influential person in the
king's royal court.

At this point, Mordechai and Haman meet for the first
time, under unpleasant circumstances for Haman. Mordechai is the only person who refuses to kneel and bow in
front of Haman. Haman becomes furious and persuades
the senseless king to issue a decree that will devastate all
the Jews in the entire kingdom.

When the disheartening tidings reach Mordechai, he puts on a sackcloth and ashes as a sign of mourning and lamenting. When Esther, the new queen, hears about Mordechai, she sends him a message to quit mourning. Mordechai refuses to listen to her. In fact, he warns her that she will not be able to escape the bitter destiny of her people despite her status in the royal court. Esther is convinced to talk to the king about his disastrous decree on behalf of the entire Jewish nation.

When Esther approaches the king, although he did not invite her (no one could see the king unless he summoned the person), he welcomes her most willingly while telling her that he will meet any wish of hers. Unexpectedly, Esther does not raise the exceedingly urgent matter of the deadly decree against all Jews and instead invites him to join Haman in a wine feast, which she wants to set in the evening.

The surprise for the reader is absolute: why does Esther fail to mention the murderous plot against her people and instead introduces such a friendly invitation, notably to Haman, her foe? This choice opens a gap that will be filled only later. In the meantime, that unfilled informative gap follows the reading process like a shadowing cloud and makcs it more tense, more intensified, and intriguing.

This is a rhetorical device that consists of suspense. That suspense becomes more intense as the unfolding text seems to abandon the wine feast issue and focuses on the king, who cannot sleep and asks for the book of the chronicles of his kingdom. In this book of chronicles, the king reads about the planned rebellion and murder plot that was unveiled by Mordechai, saving the king's life.

The king wonders why Mordechai was not bountifully rewarded. He calls for Haman and asks him how he would treat a man who finds favor in the king's eyes. Haman, believing that the king is speaking about him, suggests that such a man should be dressed in royal clothes, put on a horse's back, and led in the streets of the capital city, while the man who leads him calls loudly, "This is the way the king treats the one who finds favor in his eyes."

Haman is astounded to learn that the king had Mordechai in mind, and he is compelled to lead Mordechai in the streets of the capital city, while calling loudly that Mordechai is the one who finds favor in the eyes of the king. That deviation from the plot—while creating suspense—is neither random nor arbitrary. It reinforces the tension on the part of the reader who cannot fill the gap: will Esther meet success upon her attempt to rescue all the Jews in the Persian empire?

The plot continues unfolding, however, and the reader returns to the feast Esther is conducting for the king and Haman. At the feast, the king again asks Esther for her wish and promises to fulfill it instantly up to his entire kingdom. At that very moment, Esther takes the masquerade off Haman's face. She points at him and calls him a foe, an enemy, and evil. Haman is executed by the king's order. Also, his ten sons are executed at Esther's demand, although they had committed no iniquity. Nevertheless, the gap has not been completely filled.

The decree to annihilate all the Jews in the vast Persian empire has not been annulled. At this point of artistic climax, Esther throws herself at the king's legs, weeping, and asks him to cancel that vicious decree. Her wish is granted by the king; the Jews in the Persian kingdom are redeemed.

Naturally, the reader is encouraged to assume that this action marks the end of the plot, one that starts with a life threat upon the Jews and ends with a full redemption of the Jews. That assumption proves to be wrong, however, as an unexpected surprise (a rhetorical device) is introduced: the Jews throughout the entire Persian kingdom are permitted to kill as many gentiles as they wished. After the first day of slaughter, Esther asks the king to give the Jews one more day to slaughter as many gentiles as possible. Her wish is granted, and on that day, the Jews killed 75,000 people throughout the entire Persian kingdom.

One may wonder why such a murderous "patch" was added to the plot after it reached its climax and culmination. The only plausible way to answer that question is to view it from a moral/existential level. Accordingly, even the victimized may turn into a victimizer; even the one who was about to be slaughtered may find himself/herself slaughtering others.

In this way, the book ends with an existential-moral lesson that casts a new light upon the entire plot of the Scroll of Esther. This new light enables one to comprehend more profoundly the plot and the characters in the Scroll of Esther by introducing them from an unexpected universal perspective, one in which morality and the nature of human beings act as cornerstones.

WAS MOSES A TRAGIC HERO?

W hen Moses (*Moshe* in Hebrew; originally an Egyptian name that means "son") is traditionally associated with tragedy, it is related to the following tragic fact. Moses, the leader of the ancient Hebrews/Israelites who led the nation for forty immensely challenging years in the desert while heading for the Promised Land (initially the Land of Canaan) is not permitted (by God) to enter that Promised Land. According to the Bible, Moses shall see the Promised Land in the distance (from the summit of the Avarim Mountain), but will not be allowed to set foot there. No doubt, it is not only a tragedy upon the part of Moses, it is equally the most tormenting one.

Nevertheless, when in this chapter we relate to the tragedy of Moses, we consider primarily that tragedy from the structural point of view of ancient Greek drama. The concept of the theory of the Greek tragedy is the following. Tragedy commences when society finds itself in the midst of an agonizing calamity: barrenness, drought, misery, austerity, famine, chagrin, suffering, distress, desolation, disaster. Society is mediocre by nature. Hence society cannot redeem itself independently from its downfall, which will cure and heal it, and extricate it from its horrifying wretchedness. For the latter, there is a need for a heroic person who can bestow remedy upon a suffering society.

Such a hero is found in a mediocre society and indeed he/she eventually saves (after encountering countless challenges, tests, and stumbling blocks) the suffering society and confers upon it its desirable redemption and salvation. Nevertheless, the heroic figure is doomed to be evicted and exiled from society.

There are two formal reasons for the latter, which stem from two shortcomings of the redeeming hero. First, an emotional flaw, one that is associated with hubris, arrogance, and haughtiness. Second, an intellectual flaw: the tragic hero fails for a moment to read the writing on the wall, to decipher it and its message accurately. The Greeks called the latter *amartea*.

Behind those two formal reasons for the eviction of the heroic redeemer from society, there is the real reason: mediocre society cannot tolerate nor embrace such an individual, who is so singularly elevated, one who eclipses the intellectual and social faculties of society, one who puts society to shame. That is the very reason for the eviction of the lofty, heroic redeemer from the boundaries of a mediocre society.

Moses was such a heroic redeemer. He redeemed the Hebrew/Israelite nation from agonizing, humiliating slavery in the land of Egypt. He led his ungrateful people into the desert for forty years of suffering, hardship, and mounting obstacles. He bestowed remedy and redemption upon his society.

Nonetheless, he also suffered from two flaws, emotional and intellectual. When the people suffer from haunting thirst in the desert, Moses pleads with God, and God promises Moses that He will provide with water to quench the thirst of the people. Moses just had to talk to the closest rock and the rock will provide water bountifully. However, the thirsty people kept pressing Moses until he lost his patience. Thus he twice struck the rock with his rod and a stream of water gushed out and quenched the thirst of the people.

The latter action amalgamates both intellectual flaw (*amartea*) and the emotional flaw. Intellectually, Moses failed to comprehend to the fullest the unlimited might of God. Emotionally, Moses displayed unforgivable hubris by taking upon himself the role of God, by believing that he could replace God.

As in the Greek tragedy, those two flaws cover for the real one: Moses is compelled to be exiled from society because a mediocre society cannot tolerate and embrace such a heroic person who clouds society in all aspects.

Moses did have to go. And Moses did go, like the hero in the Greek tragedy. That is the tragedy of the Greek hero. And that was the tragedy of Moses.

DAVID THE RIDDLE:
ENIGMAS AND NON-REALISTIC EVENTS
THAT ENGULF THE CHRONICLES OF
YOUNG DAVID

Not many biblical characters are associated with so many enigmatic, non-realistic phenomena and events as young David. Those enigmas and riddle-like characteristics, which are presented when David, the shepherd boy, is introduced for the very first time in a course of biblical events and chronicles.

The prophet Samuel is instructed by God—after He rejected King Saul from kingship for failing to fulfill God's command to kill the king of the hostile, cruel Amalek people, who attacked the helpless Israelites viciously and mercilessly in the desert—to go to Jesse Bethlehemite since He already singled out among Jesse's sons the one to be the next king. Samuel the prophet arrives in Bethlehem and is presented to Jesse's seven sons. However, the chosen son was not among them.

Then Jesse sends for his youngest son, a boy named David (meaning "beloved"), who was attending his father's flocks. David appears and is described in the following fashion: "He was ruddy-cheeked, bright-eyed and good-looking" (1 Samuel, 16;12). And God says to Samuel: "Rise and anoint him since he is the one" (ibid, ibid). When Saul is approached by David, who wishes to fight the giant Philistine, Goliath, Saul calls David a boy (na'ar): "You cannot fight Goliath, as you are only a boy and he is a warrior since his young age" (1 Samuel 17;33).

After David defeats Goliath, however, Saul appoints David to be a military commander of troops: "And David with his troops met success upon launching any military mission he had to accomplish" (1 Samuel 18;5). Here is a riddle, a confusing, baffling enigma. David was a boy. Indeed, because he was a boy, he could defeat Goliath, as he could attack Goliath from a totally unexpected angle (fighting with only a sling used dexterously), one that Goliath could not predict. Hence, despite the fact that he defeated Goliath, David was still a boy, according to the biblical text.

Is it possible that a boy would become a military general who leads his troops in the battlefield while meeting nothing but a sequence of rewarding successes? That and more.

A short while later, Saul asks David to marry his oldest daughter, Meirab. When David turns down that offer, he is asked by Saul to marry his other daughter, Michal. David did marry Michal. Is it possible that a shepherd boy could marry a grown-up woman? It is as likely as a shepherd boy, who slings well, becoming a victorious warrior and military commander (while encountering spectacular success and greatness).

This is one of many cases in which the Bible gives up realistic, logical considerations and justifications to deliver a message (like, for instance, in the case of Samson, who catches three hundred foxes or slays one thousand

David the Riddle

Philistine warriors with one small jawbone of an ass.) In these unrealistic, enigmatic events in the life of young David, the biblical text aims to portray the incredibly rapid speed in which David turns into a military commander and the king's son-in-law. For the sake of depicting the swiftly growing development of young David, the realistic, logical aspect of the text is suspended, is muted.

Similar is the case of David, the lion, and the bear. When David tells Saul he wishes to fight the giant Goliath and defeat him, Saul tells David that he, David, is only a boy who cannot fight such a dangerous giant, war machine (Saul does not use these words but that is exactly what he means). To prove to Saul that he can defeat the giant Goliath, David tells the king how he fought both a lion and a bear who tried to snatch a ewe lamb from his father's flock, and how he killed both of them. A boy kills both a lion and a bear with entirely bare hands? And if such is the case, how come that no one has ever heard of it?

It brings to mind the following. When later—David is still a boy—Saul asks David to bring him one hundred foreskins of Philistines in order to marry Michal, enthusiastic David and his army kill two hundred Philistines; David then brings their foreskins to Saul and they are counted fastidiously.

Can this tale hold water? A shepherd boy who kills two hundred Philistines? Again, the message is permitted to suspend—indeed, eclipse—reality. The message here, like in previous cases, aims to focus on the speedy "metamorphosis" David experiences, transforming from a ruddy-cheeked, bright-eyed, good-looking shepherd boy to a remarkably successful military warrior who earns the admiration and loyalty of the troops he leads into battle.

In this context, it is a matter of interest to relate to the following. After David kills Goliath, he cuts off the giant's head. From that moment on, he roams about the battle-field and eventually reaches Jerusalem, Goliath's head still hanging from his hand. Even when he is brought to the royal site where King Saul sits, he still carries the head of dead Goliath in his hand. The latter fails to agree with the image of a young, ruddy-cheeked bright-eyed, handsome, innocent boy. It fits better an adult, rough warrior who does not recoil from anything, as repulsive as it may be.

Again, realism, experimental logic, are sacrificed here on the altar of the delivered message. The delivered message here is preparing the reader for the speedy

"metamorphosis" David will experience, from an innocent , sweet looking boy to a mature, mighty, tough warrior, who can bear and tolerate everything, even the most disgusting act.

When the inspiring spirit of God departs from Saul, he is haunted by an evil spirit from God. Saul's courtiers advise him to find a skillful man who plays the lyre well: whenever the evil spirit haunts Saul, he will listen to a soothing lyre music and the evil spirit will stop hounding him. One of Saul's courtiers says the following: "I have observed a son of Jesse the Bethlehmite who is skilled in music, he is a mighty fellow, a well-trained warrior, speaks well, is good looking, and God is with him" (1 Samuel, 16; 18).

This short paragraph presents some astounding riddles. A boy who is a mighty fellow? A boy who never set an eye on the battlefield is a well-trained warrior? How does the courtier know that the boy speaks well? Did he ever converse with him? And how does the courtier know that David is inspired by God? It appears that that paragraph foreshadows the characteristics of the future of a mature David. The latter is introduced so early in the text to manifest the fine qualities of David that will be presented later.

When the war between Israel and the Philistines is about to break out, Jesse, David's father, sends him to his three older brothers who are in the battlefield, and bring them some food, as well as to their commander. When David reaches the battlefield and learn about horrifying Goliath, he hears some soldiers talking about Goliath: "And the men of Israel were saying among themselves, the man who kills the giant will be bountifully rewarded by the king with great richness; he will also give him his daughter in marriage and grant exemption to his father's house in Israel" (1 Samuel, 17;25).

David hears the above discussion. Nevertheless, it seems that he does not find it enough hearing for the first time about the plentifully rich reward the king will bestow upon the one who kills Goliath.

David finds it necessary to hear that time after time. Even after he does not hear it for the next time, he keeps asking, waiting eagerly to hear again about the same promising reward. The latter casts light on one of David's unappealing characteristics: he is greedy. And also: he is shrewdly calculating, both carefully and cunningly preparing himself for a future of greatness.

One more unappealing characteristic of David presents itself in the following text: " When David finished talking to King Saul, Jonathan's soul became bound up with the soul of David; Jonathan loved David as he loved himself....and Jonathan made a pact with David as Jonathan loved David as he loved himself" (1 Samuel, 18;1-3).

Although the word "love" keeps repeating in this paragraph, it never says that David loved Jonathan, King Saul's son, only that Jonathan loved David as he loved himself. Hence David fails to reciprocate, even when it comes to his fervently loving closest friend and supporter. David, who can calculate shrewdly his steps, may find Jonathan's love for him a useful springboard from which he can launch maneuvers that will enhance his plans for the future.

Also, when Michal loves David, he fails to reciprocate. Marrying Michal, the king's daughter, was nothing but "good business" on shrewd David's part, an act that will blaze his trail to power and greatness.

The following device is very enigmatic indeed. First, David is brought to the royal palace to play his lyre for emotionally troubled Saul and to sooth this way the evil spirit that keeps haunting the king.

Later on, already on the battlefield David just reached, one reads the following enigmatic paragraph: "David was the son of a certain Ephrathite Bethlehem in Judah whose name was Jesse, and he had eight sons, and in Saul's time he was already old, advanced in years. The oldest sons of Jesse followed Saul in the war against the Philistines. The names of his three oldest sons who had gone to the war were Eliab, the first-born son, the next one Abinadab, and third Shama, and David was the youngest son" (1 Samuel, 17; 12-14).

This paragraph is most enigmatic indeed. Why does the text echo and repeat information that was previously reported in much detail? Apparently, this repetition is neither random nor arbitrary, nor one that attests to a remiss, unskillful author. When David "grows," "develops" through the plot's chronicles, this is echoed by a repeating text that symbolizes the transition of David from one stage in his development to the next, more elevated, one. As if David is "reborn." In this case, the repetition takes place when David reaches the battlefield, from which he will step higher to killing the arch foe of Israel and entering the royal court.

After David kills Goliath with only a sling and a stone, we read the following: "When Saul saw David approaching the Philistine he asked Abner, his army commander, 'Who is this boy?' and Abner responded, 'By your life, your majesty, I have no idea.' And the king told Abner to find out who is that boy." When David came to Jerusalem after defeating the Philistine, Abner took him to Saul and David still had the head of Goliath in his hand. And Saul approached David and asked him, "Who is your father?" and David said, "My father is your servant Jesse the Bethalahmite." (1 Samuel 17; 55-58).

It seems that Saul entirely forgot that he was the one who had given David the blessing prior to fighting Goliath; and he equally forgot that for quite a while now, every day,

David was playing the lyre for him, when he was haunted and terrorized by the evil spirit from God who deserted him.

Is it possible that Saul had forgotten all of that? It is not possible. Like in the previous case of repetition, the latter is introduced when David reaches a new stage in his rapidly forming, new "being," as if he is symbolically reborn, as if he is going through metamorphosis.

When Saul wants his older daughter, Merab, to marry David, he tells David the following: "Here is my older daughter, Merab; I will give her to you in marriage; in return, you will be my warrior and fight the battles of God" (1 Samuel, 18;17). That request by Saul (David will be a warrior) is quite bewildering indeed. Accordingly, Saul expresses his hope that David will fight Israel's wars while David had already done this and earned the admiration of the entire army.

That enigmatic phrase may be explained on a psychological level. Accordingly, Saul had been so excruciatingly scorched by David's military success to the point that he preferred to forget it. He wishes David to be, from now on, a warrior for the following sole purpose: "Saul thought: let not my hand strike him; let the hand of the Philistines strike him" (1 Samuel, 18;17). Ironically, in years to come, the mature David utilizes the very same murderous device by sending Uriah the Hittite to be killed in the most dangerous part of the battle-field (to capture Bathsheba, Uriah's wife, during the war against the Amonites).

When Saul offers David the chance to marry his older daughter, David responds as follows: "Who am I and what is my life—my father's family in Israel—that I would become the king's son-in-law?" (1 Samuel, 18:18). However, when Saul offers David his younger daughter, Michal, to be his wife, we read the following: "David was pleased with the idea to become the king's son in law" (1 Samuel, 18;26).

David's enthusiastic willingness to become the king's son-in-law casts ironic light on David's previous, seemingly humble exclamation, "Who am I to become the king's son-in-law?" In light of the new text, (David expresses his enthusiastic willingness to become the king's son-in-law), David's first reaction ("Who am I to become the king's son-in-law?") seems hypocritical. The text does not provide a reason for David's rejection of Merab, while preferring Michal. It is quite unclear, notably in both cases—marrying Merab, or Michal—the requested bride-price is fighting the Philistines.

Some of David unpleasant characteristics—greed, failure to reciprocate Jonathan's love for him, blazing cunningly his trail to greatness—may explain how the ruddy-cheeked, bright-eyed, handsome shepherd boy later becomes the leader of a gang of six hundred bitter, desperate, dangerous men who lived in the desert, away from the margins of society (when David runs away from Saul, who tries to kill him).

The gang (Habiru/Apiru, according to some biblical archeologists) spends most of the time in the desert, from which they launch cruel, murderous raids, such as the one targeting the Amalekites (under the shielding umbrella of Achish, the Philistine king of Gath): "When David attacked the region he would leave no man or woman alive; he would take flocks, herds, camels and clothing" (1 Samuel 27;9).

That very David, between killing and looting, also "hoards" and "accumulates" wives: Michal, Abigail, and Achinoam.

When the prophet Samuel anointed David to be king of Israel, he did it in the presence of David's older brothers (1 Samuel, 16;13), who naturally envy David. The latter is translated into fury. For example, when David's oldest brother, Eliab, sees how David speaks to soldiers on the battlefield, he scolds him with uncontrolled fury: "Why did you come down here, and with whom did you leave the flock in the wilderness? I have known your wickedness and malice..." (1 Samuel, 17:28).

That is the outcome of jealousy when the older brothers realize that their youngest brother is the chosen one, anointed to be a king. However, perhaps David himself gave some reasons to ignite such disdain and hatred. That we cannot know, that we will never know.

Nevertheless, David's older brothers' jealousy echoes the jealousy and animosity of Joseph's older brothers felt toward him. (The motif of sinful older brothers keeps repeating through the Bible: Judah's two older sons sin and are killed by God and also Naomi's two older sons die; the names of both—Machlon and Cilyon—mean morbid illness and destitution.) Indeed, Joseph's haughtiness and lack of sensitivity (forcing the brothers to listen to his arrogant dreams in which they are humiliated) helped to kindle their initial animosity towards him for being their father's the chosen one. As in the case of young David and his brothers: jealousy triggers and feeds animosity.

In light of David's some unappealing characteristics, who knows which one he practiced while interacting with his brothers before he was anointed—in the presence of his brothers—by the prophet Samuel to be the next king of Israel.

That is the story of young David. A story which is saturated with riddles, enigmas and subtext which is not less evident than the surface, "formal" text. A story which consists of bravery and greed, admiration and selfishness. All the latter, and much more, make the story of young David a vital story, a compelling story, and an enigmatic story. In short: a good story.

THE DOVE THAT DIDN'T WISH TO FLY: SATIRE, PARODY, HUMOR, AND IRONY IN THE BOOK OF JONAH

In the eighth century BCE (during the reign of the Israelite king, Jerobam the Second [783 BCE-743 BCE]), there was a prophet named Jonah Ben Amitai. However, there is no connection between the two prophets who bore the same name.

One may cogently argue that the Book of Jonah (in Hebrew, Jonah means "dove," his father's name is Amitai, which means "truthfulness") is quite outstanding among the books of the Bible since it is saturated with ramified and shrewdly molded aspects of satire, farce, absurdity, parody, humor, and irony. Indeed, satire envelopes the other aspects. It utilizes all of them to scold, to rebuke, and to teach a lesson while hoping to remedy.

Many scholars have already related to the satirical nature of the Book of Jonah.[1] Humor wishes to introduce a comic situation or character without wishing to mock or to hurt, but rather to heal natural human shortcomings.

Irony consists of two layers of meaning: the surface layer, which is like a masquerading stratum, and the latent layer, which holds the true meaning of the statement or situation.

Parody is a kind of dramatized humor that mimics and ridicules a certain character while stressing his/her shortcomings, attempting to produce remedy without putting down the subject matter.

Satire is a literary genre that enlists humor, irony, and parody in order to criticize a certain character who displays weaknesses, a "plagued" social decorum, or an entity in order to seek healing.[2]

Undoubtedly, the Book of Jonah introduces a character, the prophet Jonah, who deserves the most piercing satire since he is childish, cowardly oriented, devoid of logic, pathetic, obnoxious, and more than once willing to contest God's way of operation. At the same time, Jonah finds himself in the most absurd situations and displays senseless behavior, pitiful childishness, and ridiculous trains of thought. All of these factors produce a pattern of frustrated expectations, since there is an unbridgeable gap between what one justly expects from a prophet and the way in which Jonah practices his prophecy.

The very first time the reader encounters him, Jonah is commanded by God to go to the sinful city Nineveh and proclaim its forthcoming destruction. Jonah's reaction is absolutely absurd: he travels to the city of Jaffa and goes down in a ship while sailing to the city of Tarshish in order to escape from God. In this short paragraph, the verb *laredet*, which means "to go down" or "to descend," is mentioned twice (and later one more time), stressing the derogative connotations associated with that word. The word choice in effect scolds Jonah for running away from God's mission (while being so childish as to believe that God will fail to track him down wherever he goes).

When a tempest breaks out at sea and all the sailors desperately struggle and implore their pagan gods for help, Jonah, in the most unbelievably stoic serenity, goes down (again the verb *laredet* with the negative connotations) to the depths of the ship and falls asleep in perfect tranquility. That senseless behavior mocks Jonah, who is rebuked by the captain of the ship, and also exhibits his childishness since metaphorically he acts like an embryo in his mother's womb.

Similar metaphors appear two more times in the Book of Jonah: when he finds himself in the belly of the big fish and when he enters the booth he built while facing Nineveh. In all three cases, he is metaphorically portrayed as an embryo seeking shielding shelter in his mother's womb. In this way, Jonah's childishness, which is at odds with his mission as a prophet, stands out and gains the reader's attention.

Another characteristic of Jonah is his death wish. When the ship is about to break apart and sink to the bottom of the tempestuous sea because of his disobedience of God's commandment, Jonah asks the sailors to throw him into the deadly, raging waves. When he comes out of the big fish, he appears to be reborn. (It is interesting to note that the male fish turns into a female fish at that time, as if it is giving birth to Jonah.)

When Jonah finds out that God accepted the repentance of the sinful people of Nineveh, Jonah is grieved to the point that he seeks death. Accordingly, he says to God: "And now God take away my soul from me as I better be dead than alive" (Jonah 4;4). When the great plant that God provided as protection for Jonah withers, Jonah seeks death again: "He wishes he would be dead and said I better die than live" (ibid., 4;8).

There is a touch of piercing farce in all these death wishes of Jonah's: there is no proportion between what happens to him and his extreme reaction. In addition, his death wish contradicts the Jewish credo formulated in Deuteronomy 30;19: "And I gave you life and death...and you should choose life so you shall live." Hence Jonah, the prophet, who is expected to represent God's rules, acts against one of the most crucial rules of God.

The childishness of Jonah is further reinforced by his reaction to God's decision to grant forgiveness to the people of Nineveh after they repent. Jonah grieves bitterly, becomes upset that God did not fulfill his prophecy (the one from which he ran away), and behaves like a little child whose toy was taken. Also, as previously noted, Jonah's childishness manifested itself in his constant quest for a womb: the depths of the ship, the fish's belly, and the booth. That quest is equally comic and absurd.

The "speed of light" with which the people of Nineveh repent—covering not only themselves but also their domestic beasts with sackcloth—is also tinged with humor. Their repentance seems quite superficial, one that is not candidly practiced, but rather formed from the basic instinct of a desire to live. In light of the latter, it is neither arbitrary nor random that God Himself mocks the repenting people of Nineveh by relating to them as people who "fail to tell the difference between right and left" (ibid., 4;11).

In this respect, there is an intriguing analogy between the childish, absurd prophet Jonah and the childish, absurd people of Nineveh: all of them act illogically, all of them act in an absurd fashion, and all of them obey their basic, primitive instincts instead of obeying plausible logic and divine faith.

The parody and satire in the book of Jonah reach their very vertex as Jonah is found analogous to the sinful people at whom he directs a prophecy of destruction. Now the reader can comprehend to the fullest the irony that is present in the name Jonah, son of Amitai. Jonah, a dove, a symbol of peace, is seeking peace while the biblical Jonah refuses to tolerate the peace earned through the repentance of the people of Nineveh.

Amitai, truthfulness, is at odds with the prophet Jonah, who runs away from the truth, who fails to tell the difference between truthful reality and his basic, childish instincts as the senseless people of Ninveh fail to tell the difference between left and right. Hence the prophet whose names are associated with peace and truthfulness does not deserve either of them.

NOTES

1. Among the scholarly works that relate to satire, parody, irony, and humor in the book of Jonah are the following:

> *Green, Abraham. "Satire in the Book of Jonah." JSOT 21 (1981): 59-81.

> *Simon, Uriel. *The JPS Bible Commentary: Jonah.* Philadelphia: JPS, 1999.

> *Carry, Philip. *Jonah.* New York: Brzzos Press, 2008.

> *Sharp, Carolyn J. *Irony and Meaning in the Hebrew Bible.* Bloomington: Indiana University Press, 2009.

> *Freidman, Hershey H. "Is There Humor in the Hebrew Bible?" *Humor: International Journal of Humor Research* 15, no.2 (2002): 215-222.

> *Green, Barbra. *Jonah's Journeys.* California: Liturgical Press, 2005.

> *Whedbee, J. William. *The Bible and the Comic Vision.* Cambridge: Cambridge University Press, 2002.

> *Milles, John A. Jr. "Laughing in the Bible: Jonah and Parody." *Jewish Quarterly Review* 65 (1975): 81-168.

2. Cf. Preminger, Alex. *Princeton Encyclopedia of Poetry and Poetics.* Princeton: Princeton University Press, 1974. Rivlin, Asher *Lexicon of Literature.* Tel Aviv: Sifriyat Poalim, 1978 (in Hebrew).

WHY DID SARAH LAUGH? AND WHY DID SAMPSON LAUGH? AND WHY DID JOSEPH NOT LAUGH?

The verb *li-tzchok* or *le-tzachek* in the Bible seems to be one of the most misleading verbs. On the one hand, it means "to laugh" in modern Hebrew. While the letters "tz" are converted into "s," it also means "to play." (In the *binyan*/pattern of conjugation, *pa'al li-tzchok* means to laugh, while in *binyan*/pattern of conjugation *pi'el le-sachek* means to play.) We will realize, however, that there is a causal semantic connection between the two. Nevertheless, *li-tzchok* in the Bible and perhaps primarily *le-tzachek*, also possess sexual connotations. The latter can be positive ones, ones which are associated with fertility and negative ones, ones associated with unworthy sexual activity.

The name *Yitzchak* (Isaac) is a good example for connecting the verb *li-tzchok* with positive connotations, ones associated with fertility. God delivers to Abraham the unexpected tiding that in his old age (both his and Sarah's) they will conceive a son, his name should be *Yitzchak* ("Isaac"): "And I will maintain my covenant with him as an everlasting covenant for his offspring to come" Genesis 17;19).

In this case, the name *Yitzchak* obviously reflects the positive connotations associated with the verb *li-tzchok*, related to fertility, to life. Indeed, we read the following about Abraham: "Abraham threw himself on his face and laughed as he said to himself, 'Can a child be born to a man a hundred years old, or can Sarah bear a child at ninety?' (ibid, 17).

Here, Abraham's laughter is devoid of sexual connotations, although it is still associated with fertility, with life. His laughter stems from disbelief, from surprise, and even from distrust. Nevertheless, God does not take offense. However, when Sarah laughs for the same reason (ibid, 18;12), she is scolded by God, "Why did Sarah laugh? saying 'Shall I in truth bear a child, old as I am?' Is anything too wondrous for God?" (ibid, 18;12).

Abraham is not rebuked for Sarah's distrusting laughter because Abraham, not Sarah, is the chosen prophet of God, and what he can do, Sarah cannot.

The verb *li-tzchok* or *le-tzachek* can be associated with sexual connotations while being devoid of the meaning of fertility. For instance, in Genesis 26, we read the following: "When Abimelech, King of the Philistines, looking out of the window, saw Isaac fondling (*metzachek*) his wife Rebekah, Abimelech sent for Isaac and said, "So she is your wife. Why then did you say, 'She is my sister'"?

Isaac said to him, "Because I feared I might lose my life on account of her."

Abimlech said, "What have you done to us? One of the people might have lain with your wife and you have brought guilt upon all of us." (Ibid, 26;8-10)

Why did Sarah Laugh?

Nevertheless, in most of the cases, the verb *le-tzachek* or *li-tzchok* is clearly connected to derogatory sexual connotations. When Sarah sees "the son whom Hagar the Egyptian has born to Abraham *metzachek*, she said to Abraham, "Cast out that slave woman and her son [Hagar and Ishmael], for the son of that slave shall not share in the inheritance with my son Isaac" (Genesis 21;9-10).

What did Ishmael do that ignited so fervently Sarah's rage? Why did she talk about inheritance? Why did she demand that Abraham evict Hagar and Ishmael?

Ishmael was *metzachek*. This way, Ishmael innocently displayed his sexual maturity (he was at least fourteen years old), and being the first-born son of Abraham, he cast a shadow on Isaac's exclusive portion of Abraham's inheritance as Abraham's chosen heir. Hence, it was Ishmael's sexual maturity (*metzachek*) that kindled Sarah's fury by threatening to perhaps eclipse the beloved and only son, Isaac.

When the people of Israel are waiting impatiently for Moses to come down from the mountain of God, they put pressure on Aaron to sculpt the Golden Calf, which they began worshipping. Aaron also built an altar (perhaps to compensate for the sculpting of the Golden Calf), declared a holiday in honor of God, and "early the next day, the people offered up burnt offerings and brought sacrifices of well-being; they set down to eat and drink and then rose *le-tzachek* (Exodus 32; 4-6). Undoubtedly, the verb *le-tzachek* in this context means a certain festive activity engaged with unworthy sexual manifestation. The derogatory meaning of the sexual *le-tzachek* in this context is very evident indeed.

In the Book of Judges (Chapter 16), we read about the
tragic downfall of Samson (although he was the one
blamed for that calamity in his life): his hair is shaved, he
completely loses his wondrous power, his eyes are gouged
out by the cheering Philistines, he is shackled in bronze
fetters, and he becomes a mill slave in a dungeon. The
Philistines' vulgar happiness and brutal satisfaction have
no limits. They start yelling: "Call Samson here and let
him *le-tzachek* in front of us; and they brought blind
Samson from the dungeon and he *va-yetzachek* in front of
them... and the temple of their god, Dagon, was full of men
and women and there were some three thousand men and

women on the roof watching Samson in his *tzchok* (ibid, 25;27). It is not quite clear in what way Samson was forced to *le-tzachek* in front of the thousands of cheering Philistines, intoxicated by the brutal happiness of revenge.

One thing is clear, however. The way Samson was compelled to *le-tzachek* was associated with humiliating sexual connotations. Samson had lost his legendary strength and was forced to *le-tzachek*.

In Genesis Chapter 39, we read about Joseph, who was sold to Potiphar, a respected courtier of Pharaoh and his chief steward. Joseph earns God's blessing and becomes immensely successful, to the point that his new master "left all that he had in Joseph's hands and, with him there, he paid attention to nothing save the food that he ate" (ibid., 6).

However, Potiphar's wife lusted after the young, handsome Joseph. She kept trying to tempt him, time after time, but he refused to commit such an iniquity against his faithful master. "One such day, he came into the house to do his work. None of the household being there inside, she caught Joseph by his garment and said, 'lie with me.' But he left his garment in her hand and he fled outside. She called out to her servants and said to them, 'Look, he had to bring us a Hebrew *le-tzachek* with us and then he approached me, aiming to lie with me, but I screamed loudly. And when he heard me screaming at the top of my voice, he left his garment with me and got away and fled outside" (ibid., 11-15).

Clearly, she summoned her servants and told them her viciously deceitful version of the situation, in case one of them had witnessed or heard what was really going on.

The Cryptic Bible

She wanted to make sure her deceitful version was the accepted one. Later on, when Potiphar, her husband and Joseph's master, returns home, she repeats her deceitful version, blaming her husband for bringing a "Hebrew slave *le-tzachek* with me" (ibid., 17).

Potiphar's fury was very great indeed and he orders Joseph to the pit/dungeon (the motif of a "pit" continues to haunt the innocent Joseph since his brothers cast him into a pit in the desert). The derogatory, sexual connotations associated here with the verb *le-tzachek* call for no further interpretation.

Hence, Sarah did laugh. She was associated with "*li-tzchok*" at her choice. Her *li-tzchok* was associated with the sexual connotations engaged with fertility.

Samson was compelled to laugh, *le-tzachek*, in the most humiliating, sexually oriented fashion.

Joseph, who refused to laugh, *le-tzachek*, to have sex with his master's wife, paid dearly for that respectful refusal.

In all cases, *li-tzchok*, *le-tzachek*, "to laugh," have sexual connotations, which are like the double face of Janus, the two-faced mythological Roman figure: good and evil, fertility and lust, welcome sexuality (that yields fertility), and obscene, detestable sexuality.

Hence, both Sarah and Samson did laugh, while Joseph did not.

A TALE OF TWO SPIES
AND ONE HARLOT—
ISRAELI SPIES IN JERICHO

In the Book of Joshua, at the very beginning of the second chapter, one reads the following: "Joshua, son of Nun, secretly sent two spies from Shittim, saying 'Go, reconnoiter the land and the city of Jericho.' So they set out, and they came to the house of a harlot named Rahab and they lay there."

The dense irony that is inlaid in this short volume of text can neither be missed nor denied. While the two spies are instructed to scout the country and the city of Jericho, they do none of that. Instead, they find themselves in the house of a harlot, and their activities there are saturated with sexual connotations: they came, they lay.

The verb "to come" (*la-voh*) is commonly used in the Bible to mean sexual intercourse. For instance, we read in Genesis 16;4 that Abraham came to Hagar and she conceived. And Judah came to Tamar (*va-yavoh*) and she conceived (Genesis 38;18) Most certainly, such is the meaning of the verb "to lie" (to cohabit, *li-shkav*), notably when both verbs come together as in the case of the David and Bathsheba: "David *came* to Bathsheba and *lay* with her and she bore a son" (Samuel 2;12, 24).

The irony that derives from the activities—indeed, as well as from the lack of activities—of the two spies could not be more piercingly mocking. They are instructed to tour the land and notably the city of Jericho, and instead they limit their mission to visiting a whorehouse, where they apparently indulge themselves with sexual activity.

The spies continue to fall short of their mission. They were instructed to act "secretly" (*cheresh*), but they shamefully fail in this department as well. Accordingly, the very evening they reach the harlot Rahab's house, their secret mission turns into public knowledge: "It was told to the king of Jericho that people from the Israelites arrived in the evening to spy out the land" (Joshua 2;2). When the arrival of the spies became known to the king of Jericho, he sent his order to Rahab the harlot: "Produce the men who came to you and entered your house, for they have come to spy out the entire land" (ibid., 2;3). Little did he know that they were preoccupied with other activities than spying.

For her own calculated reasons, Rahab disobeys the king's order and hides the two Israelites near the roof under some stalks of flax. In addition, she leads astray the king's soldiers, who were searching for the Israelites, by telling them the spies had already left and suggesting they chase them in the open.

After the soldiers leave, she tells the two hidden spies that she and everyone else knows that the Israelites are mighty in battle, that their God is undefeated, and that they will conquer the land like fire consuming a field of dry grass. Hence, she is aware that Jericho will be conquered and she asks that her life and her family's lives be spared.

Now the reader finds out the motive behind Rahab's risky efforts to protect the two spies. They agree that when Jericho is assaulted by the Israelites, she will hang a crimson cord from the window of her house, which is the along the town's wall. Her family will find refuge in her house, and their lives will be spared. The text introduces an intriguing juxtaposition. While the spies do not spy, the pagan harlot displays wholehearted trust in the Hebrew God.

To avoid the king's warriors pursuing them, the spies hide in the mountains at Rahab's instruction. Thus, instead of spying on Jericho as they had been ordered, they continue hiding. That and more. The spies richly deserve to be mocked. Time after time, they prove to be pathetically disconnected from reality. Time after time, they tell Rahab not to disclose their secretive mission, while their secret is already public knowledge.

The mocking irony aimed at the two spies continues to run its course. The two spies return to Joshua and share with him the following report: "God has delivered the whole land into our power; in fact, all the inhabitants of the land are quaking before us" (ibid., 2;24).

Their bold report is not based on serious detective work as one may expect, but rather on the testimony of one pagan harlot (although a good-hearted one) they met at random and who probably provided them with sexual services.

THE DEATH OF INNOCENCE: THE SCROLL OF RUTH

Even though the Scroll of Ruth starts with the phrase, "At the time of the Judges" (1,200 BCE–1,000 BCE), it is quite likely that it was composed in the fifth century BCE, after the destruction of the Kingdom of Judah and the first Solomon Temple and the exile to Babylon (586 BCE). The latter seems to be reasonably plausible based on the evident influence of the Aramaic language on the Hebrew language in the Scroll of Ruth.

Aramaic was the language of the Babylonian empire, to which many of the inhabitants of the Kingdom of Judah—mostly the intelligentsia, who could initiate and launch a rebellion—were exiled. It is believed that some parts of the Bible were composed during the Babylonian exile.

It is quite common to consider the Scroll of Ruth an idyll that yields a serene, pastoral, and even romantic atmosphere. The plot, the descriptions, and the dialogues unfold in a moderate, curbed fashion. Nevertheless, a close reading of the idyll may discern a tense gap between the tranquil surface and a tragic nucleus of the text.

The leading argument of this chapter is to show how the Scroll of Ruth is not as idyllic as one may assume upon *prima vista*, nor are some of its protagonists innocent. Indeed, the very beginning of the Scroll of Ruth plausibly attests to the latter. It starts with a historical framework: "In the days when the judges ruled..." (ibid. 1;1). The period of the Judges in the chronicles of Judah and Israel was notoriously known as a tempestuous period of national upheaval, distress, social calamities, lawless atmosphere, raids, looting, political chaos, and religious anarchy.

The next issue mentioned in the first phrase is the famine in the land of Judah that compelled Naomi, her husband, Elimelech, and their two sons, Machlon and Cilyon, to wander to the land of Moab. Elimelech eventually dies. The names of the two sons bring to mind disasters: Machlon is related to *machalah*, illness, while Cilyon is related to *clayah*, devastation. (Compare this to Joseph's sinful older brothers, David's hateful older brothers, Judah's sinful sons, and Samuel's sinful sons.) Hence, there is nothing idyllic here.

When Naomi and her daughter-in-law, Ruth, return to Naomi's homeland, Bet-Lechem Judah, we read the following: "When they arrived in Bet-Lechem, the whole city buzzed with excitement over them. The women said, 'Can this be Naomi?' 'Do not call me Naomi,' Naomi replied, 'call me the bitter one (*marah*) since God has made my lot very bitter; I went away full and the Lord has brought me back bitter'" (ibid., 1;21-22). Did Naomi leave Judah (the country) while being "full"? No. Indeed, she left Judah due to an oppressive calamity, famine. Hence the tragic nucleus of the Scroll of Ruth is painfully far from being latent as it is introduced in the very beginning of the scroll on the very surface layer of the text.

The first encounter between Ruth and Boaz, one of the richest men of the town, is evidently innocent. He lets her to glean and gather among the sheaves as much as she wants, and he makes sure that nobody will trouble her and that she can drink and eat as much as she wishes. When Naomi learns about the generous, compassionate way Boaz treated Ruth, she tells Ruth with much thankfulness and relief that Boaz is a relative of her family and one of her redeeming kinsmen, meaning he is the next in line to marry her after she lost her husband.

Then Naomi starts plotting her plan. She instructs Ruth to bathe, to anoint herself, to dress up in a fine dress, to go at night to the barn where Boaz is spending the night, to lie down at his feet, and to uncover his feet. Ruth responds willingly and follows Naomi's instructions. Indeed, Boaz was more than pleased to find a young, attractive woman lying at his feet in the dead of night.

The subtle text shares with the reader the dialogue between the two but not their deeds. In this way, Ruth becomes an obedient partner of Naomi in setting the plot that will "trap" Boaz and make him marry Ruth. Both Ruth and Naomi (who have no source of income) will benefit bountifully from such an alliance.

The latter is manifested in the following text: "So Boaz married Ruth; she became his wife and he cohabited with her. The Lord let her conceive, and she bore a son. And the women said to Naomi: Blessed be the Lord, who has not withheld a redeemer from you today. May his name be perpetuated in Israel. He will renew your life and sustain your old age for he is born of your daughter-in-law who loves you and better to you than seven sons" (ibid., 4;13-15).

Thus, behind the seemingly innocent idyll, which is already "plagued" by the death of Naomi's husband and her two sons (who carried names that are associated with disaster) and famine, there is a cunning plot to "snare" a rich man while practicing shrewd sexuality. This is the scroll of Ruth. And this is the death of innocence.

WHO IS AFRAID OF THE TOWER OF BABEL?

The story of the Tower of Babel is quite questionable in terms of both its content, as well as by the lesson it aims to teach. It starts by stating: "Everyone on earth had the same language and the same words" (Genesis 11;1).

Everyone? The entire population? Did the latter grow so rapidly after the devastating flood? Apparently, that population was not very vast since one valley—the valley in the Land of Shinar—could accommodate the entire population. Indeed, the text adopts the limited viewpoint of those people who wrongly believe that they are the only people in the world. Those people decided to build a town and a very high tower with its roof in the sky. In this way, they would make a name for themselves and avoid being scattered all over the world.

One may introduce the following questions: What is the connection between that tower and the fact that its builders spoke one language? Isn't it a given? When, for instance, a tower is erected in Sweden, isn't it a given that the builders speak Swedish (even if the mother tongue of some of them is not Swedish)? And how would that erected tower prevent the undesirable scattering of some of the population (perhaps most of it) all over the world? What is

W.J. LINTON

the tower, a lighthouse that prevents ships from going astray in an obscure, stormy ocean?

It appears, however, that this perplexing story has roots in tangible reality. For example, 5,000 years ago the Babylonians built tall towers from bricks made of burnt clay. The description of the way the Tower of Babel was built includes: "let us make bricks and burn them hard" (ibid., 11;3). By building such a structure, the Babylonians wished to get closer to the distant stars and learn about their destiny and future from those stars.

Whatever was in the minds of the builders of the Tower of Babel, they neither intended nor wished to challenge God or to threaten Him in any fashion or form whatsoever. They wished to stay united and they believed that the tall tower would keep them united, as they were united by the very same language that all of them shared and spoke. Such a concern, such a wish, as questionable and shaky as it may be, is perfectly legitimate and cannot be interpreted differently.

God, however, thought differently: "The Lord came down to look at the city and tower that man had built and the Lord said: If, as one people with one language for all, this is how they have begun to act, then nothing that they may propose to do will be out of their reach. Let us, then, go down and confound their speech there, so that they shall not understand one another's speech." (ibid., 11;5)

It is interesting to note that in the Bible, verbal faculties may be associated with creation. Abram turns into Abraham, Sarai turns into Sarah, and Jacob turns into Israel because they are newly "created," or elevated to a higher sphere of existence. Adam names the animals and becomes a verbal creator, and such is the case when he twice names his wife, *Isha* (woman) and *Eve/Chavah*. (The name *Chavah* derives from *chai*, "alive," as she was the first mother of all living human beings: *em kol chai*.) In the case of the Tower of Babel, verbal faculties are associated with destruction, and by God Himself.

God's reaction to the tower is indeed a matter of disturbing curiosity. Is it possible that God, who created the entire universe, the sky, the earth, all kinds of vegetation and animals, and of course, human beings, is the very same God who demolished all sinful human beings and all animals in the devastating flood? (Why? Were the animals also corrupt? In what way? And what about infants, babies, and children? Did they also commit iniquities?) Is it likely that such an unbelievably mighty God would feel threatened by one single tower made of clay bricks?! Does it make sense?

It seems, however, that the fact that God feels challenged by a single tall tower erected by the survivors of the flood does surrender and manifest God's weakness, or lack of self-confidence.

The fact that in the flood, God demolished all human beings (it is quite likely that at least a few of them were not corrupt, certainly not the infants, babies, or children), as well as all beasts of the field and birds of the sky and creeping creatures, does not attest to the might of God. On the contrary, it reflects His weaknesses, His lack of self-confidence, His tendency to be trigger-happy and shoot from the hip.

At the end of the Tower of Babel episode, we read the following: "Thus the Lord scattered them from there over the face of the whole earth and they stopped building the city [because their speech had been confounded].

That is why it was called Babel, because there the Lord confound the speech of the whole earth; and from there the Lord scattered them over the face of the whole earth" (ibid., 11;8-9).

Who's Afraid of the Tower of Babel?

One must realize that the name Babel derives from the Hebrew root *b.l.l.*, which means to confound, to mix up, to confuse, to muddle, to baffle. The name, however, is no less enigmatic. We just read the city and tower were deserted by the builders when they lost their verbal

177

common denominator and correspondingly, lost their capacity to communicate and to cooperate.

What is the point of giving a name to a city that does not exist anymore? Perhaps, to act in the capacity of a "signpost," to alert future generations about the disheartening destiny of those who dare to challenge God and doubt His superiority. And what about the weakness of God—His lack of self-confidence—demonstrated in the Tower of Babel story? This question is still awaiting a cogent, logical answer.

GOD, MOSES, AND EGYPT:
IN THE NAME OF
UNSOLVED MYSTERIES

C hapters three and four in the book of Exodus unfold the first appearance of God to Moses (from the burning, unconsumed bush), God's command to Moses to go to Pharaoh and order him to free the Israelite slaves, the wonders that God instructs Moses to perform to convince the elders of Israel that God indeed manifested Himself to Moses, Moses' doubts that he is the right person to be God's chosen agent (he fears that he does not speak well) and Aaron, Moses' brother, who joins Moses as his spokesman upon meeting with Pharaoh.

In these two chapters, the reader is told about three wonders that Moses performs while being instructed by God: turning a rod into a snake, and back to a rod; making his hand as white as leprosy and then curing it instantly; pouring water from the Nile on dry ground and turning it into blood. These three wonders should help Moses to convince both Pharaoh and the elders of Israel that he is indeed the national leader chosen by God.

The chronicles mentioned above include some "sub-stories." That and more. These "sub-stories" are indeed mysteries that cannot be solved.

The first one is the following. God shares with Moses that once the Israelites are freed from slavery, God will lead them "to a good and spacious land, a land flowing with milk and honey, the land of the Canaanites, the Hittites, the Amorites, the Hivites, the Perizzites, and the Jebusites" (Exodus 3; 8). This promise later repeats: "I will take you out of the misery of Egypt to the land of the Canaanites, the Hittites, the Amorites, the Hivites, the Perizzites, and the Jebusites, to a land flowing with milk and honey" (Exodus 3;17).

The reason the promise repeats may be explained by the wish to make that divine promise as convincing as possible. And the reason that the promise repeats in an opposite order of presentation may be explained by the wish to avoid rigidity, to yield flexibility. One may also cogently argue that mentioning in this divine promise the many peoples who already populate the Promised Land, is to let the Israelites know that the Promised Land will not be endowed upon them on a silver platter, but rather on a platter of "blood, sweat and tears." However, what is the reason of notifying tormented, oppressed, spiritless slaves that they will have to fight viciously and die for that Promised Land?

Can't such prophecy wait until the Israelites gain some strength, both physical and mental, that will help them to cope more effectively with the discouraging tidings regarding the Promised Land? What is the point of notifying them of such a challenging ordeal when they are still broken, both physically and mentally? Hence, the latter can be considered an unsolved "mystery," one that cannot be deciphered by the biblical text or by realistic logic.

God, Moses, and Egypt

The following example seems quite marginal. Nevertheless, it does reflect the leading trend of groundlessness, of unrealistic events and chronicles that are devoid of logic and therefore are justly considered unsolved mysteries.

"Moses went back to his father-in-law Jethro the Prince of Midian, and said to him 'let me go back to my kinsfolk in Egypt and see how they are faring'; and Jethro said to Moses, 'Go in peace'. God said to Moses in Midian, 'Go back to Egypt, for all the men who sought to kill you are dead'" (Exodus 4;18-19). After Moses decided to go back to Egypt, after Moses earned the consent of his father-in-law that he would go back to Egypt, does God suddenly appear and direct Moses to return to Egypt, after Moses already was on his way to Egypt. What is the logical reason God commands Moses to do something he is already doing? Perhaps it is a "tiny" mystery. However, it is still an unresolved mystery.

The next "sub-stories" are no less enigmatic. When God commands Moses to go back to Egypt, He says the following: "Go back [from Midian] to Egypt, for all the men who sought to kill you are dead" (Exodus 4;19). All the men? Who are those many men? According to the previous text, only Pharaoh "sought to kill Moses" when he learned that Moses killed an Egyptian taskmaster and buried him in the sand (Exodus 2;15). Where did those many men come from? Indeed, they never existed. A mystery.

"Pharaoh said to the Hebrew midwives, one of them was named Shiphrah and the other Puah, "when you deliver the Hebrew women, look at the birth stool, if it is a boy, kill him and if it is a girl, let her live'" (Exodus, 3;15-16). Only two midwives for the entire nation of Israel, which is portrayed as "numerous," "enormous," "prolific," "fertile"? It makes no sense. Here the biblical text twists the arm of logical reality to deliver a message (or to act in congruence of its leading trends). In this case, mentioning only two Israelite midwives makes the story more personal, easier to relate to.

After the encounter with the two Israelite midwives, one reads the following: "Then Pharaoh charged all his people, 'every boy that is born you shall throw into the Nile, but let every born girl live'" (Exodus 1;22). Something is wrong. Pharaoh is commanding the Egyptians to throw into the Nile every newborn Egyptian boy? That command fits Pharaoh's command to the Israelites, not Pharaoh's OWN people! The text does not provide with any answer to that bewildering "sub-story." A mistake by the person/people who wrote or copied this text? Perhaps this is the case.

But what is the case? How should the correct text read? A mystery.

The following text appears to be equally confusing and mysterious:

"And I (God) will dispose the Egyptians favorably toward the Israelites, so when the Israelites will be leaving Egypt, not to return, they will not go away empty-handed. Each woman will borrow from her neighbor and lodger in her house objects of gold, silver and fine clothing, and the Israelites will put those fine clothing on their sons and daughters, thus stripping the Egyptians" (Exodus 3;21-22).

This short "story" includes and displays more than one question mark. First, how come God "educates" the Israelites to exploit their neighbor Egyptians? On a level of morality, such a "lesson" is both disturbing and questionable. On top of it, it is not likely that the oppressive taskmasters who tormented the Israelite slaves resided next to their tortured slaves. After all, the Israelite/Hebrew slaves were the poorest, who lived in the poorest neighborhood, one that did not fit a higher social class, such as that of the taskmasters.

This means that God guides the Israelites to take advantage and exploit their poor Egyptian neighbors, since only poor Egyptians would reside next to slaves. And those poor Egyptian neighbors of the Israelite slaves had neither hurt nor bothered the Israelites. Only the taskmasters were the oppressors, not the Israelites' neighbors.

The latter account, however, gives rise to another enigmatic matter. Since the Egyptians who resided next to Israelite slaves could be only the very poor ones, those who belonged to the lowest level of society ranking, how do they come to possess "objects of gold and silver and fine clothing"? It makes no sense, it is absolutely devoid of logic. Hence, it is one more unsolved mystery.

The next and last unsolved mystery is exhibited in the following short "story": "While Moses was on his way to the encampment, God encountered him and sought to kill him. So Tzipora [Moses' wife] took a flint and cut off her son's foreskin, and touched his legs, saying 'you are truly a bridegroom of blood to me'. And God let Moses go, she added 'a bridegroom of blood of the circumcision'" (Exodus 4;24-25).

Does God truly intend to kill Moses, his chosen prophet, the "anointed" leader of the chosen people? Does this make sense? If Moses did not circumcise his first-born son (as understood according to this tiny "story"), could not God call Moses' attention to this negligence, and urge him to correct that with no delay, instead of aiming to slay him? From any possible angle one may address this tiny "story," will one fail to decipher its enigmatic nature. Also this tiny story remains an unsolved mystery.

From a logical perspective, the unsolved mysteries provided by these two chapters may be considered a bit disturbing. From an aesthetic, artistic perspective, however, those cases, chronicles, and events of unresolved mystery, bestow upon the text attractive vitality and desirable complexity.

WHEN JOSEPH MEETS TAMAR: A CASE OF CONFUSING COMPOSITION IN THE STORY OF JOSEPH IN EGYPT

The story of Joseph in Egypt is one of the most compelling stories in the Bible. Joseph was the most beloved son of Jacob (next to Benjamin), who sewed for him an ornamented tunic (also known, in English translation, as "a coat of many colors"; a literal translation of the Hebrew is "a tunic of stripes," *ktonet passim*). Joseph proved, however, to be not only the most beloved son, but also a haughty dreamer (as discussed previously).

One time, he dreamed that he and his ten elder brothers were binding sheaves in the field and suddenly, his sheaf rose up and stayed erect and the sheaves of the brothers bowed down to it. The brothers who envied Joseph for being the most beloved son of Jacob, turned to hate him even more bitterly for his haughty dream in which they are "portrayed" as his slaves. The brothers' fury further increased because Joseph tarnished them while bringing bad reports to Jacob, their father, behind their backs.

It is a matter of piercing irony that when Joseph reaches greatness in Egypt and the brothers descend to

Egypt to procure rations, Joseph unfairly blames them for being spies while he was, in fact, the only spy among them.

Joseph's second dream is even more arrogant. In the second dream, Joseph is surrounded by the sun, the moon, and eleven stars, which bow low to him. The sun stands for his father, the moon stands for his mother, and the eleven stars represent his eleven older brothers. It is a matter of obtrusive interest that Dina, the only daughter of Jacob and Leah, is NEVER mentioned (only when she is raped)! This is one more sad demonstration of how the Bible treats women both unfairly and poorly.

This time Jacob interferes by angrily scolding his beloved son for his blatant hubris. Later, however, Joseph's father sends him to find out how the brothers and the flocks pasturing in Dotan are faring. When the brothers see him a from afar, they conspire to kill him. However, one brother, Reuben, persuades them to withdraw from their murderous plot and instead, cast Joseph into a deep pit (having in mind to later restore Joseph to their father).

At that time, a caravan of Ishmaelite (also called Midianite) merchants was passing by and the brothers sold Joseph to those merchants. The latter arrived in Egypt and sold Joseph to a highly influential courtier in the court of Pharaoh. The name of Joseph's new master was Potiphar. Undoubtedly, this is dramatic turning point in the Joseph's destiny. What will happen to him in a new, strange country in which he becomes a slave to such a powerful master? Will his destiny continue to be bleak and murky or perhaps he will experience a soothing relief in his new, enslaving country?

When Joseph Meets Tamar

In that moment of extreme tension and anxiety in the reading process, the reader may be immensely surprised to encounter a totally different story—the story of Judah and his daughter-in-law, Tamar—which interrupts Joseph's story. Most certainly, the interest of the reader is considerably ignited. What is so special in the new story that justifies severing the story of Joseph at such a dramatic, anxious point? What may be the connection between those two extremely different stories? The new story narrates as follows.

Judah parted from his brothers and made his new dwelling place next to one already possessed by Hiram, the Adullamite. Judah married there the daughter of a Canaanite man and she bore to him three sons: *Er* (meaning in Hebrew energetic, active), *Onan* (meaning in Hebrew might, strength) and *Shelah* (meaning in Hebrew tranquility), to whom she gave birth in *kezif*, or in Hebrew, deceitfulness. The latter will be found of master interest.

The eldest son, Er, was sinful and God killed him. He left his young wife, Tamar (meaning "palm tree" in Hebrew). According to Hebrew law, the brother who is next in line, in this case, Onan, was expected to marry the widow, be intimate with her, and produce children. Onan, however, while realizing that any children would be considered his dead brother's children, did not complete the act of intimacy with his sister-in-law (he practiced *coitus interruptus*), and wasted his sperm on the floor. (The noun "onanism" follows the same noun in Hebrew [*onenut*] and derives etymologically from Onan's behavior).

God was displeased with Onan and killed him as well. Indeed, next in line was Shelah, the youngest brother.

However, his father, Judah, feared that he would die while being married to Tamar, like his two brothers, and did not give Shelah to Tamar as a husband. According to his instruction, she returned to her father's home and waited there until Shelah grew up.

Indeed, Judah did not intend to keep his word, since he feared that Shelah's destiny would echo his brothers' fate while being married to their widow, Tamar. It is a matter of interest that when Judah's wife gave birth to Shelah, she did it in *kezif,* "deceit" in Hebrew. Judah was deceitful upon addressing Tamar in the case of Shelah, his youngest son.

Tamar, however, realized the true reason for Judah's decision not to let her marrying Shelah, his youngest son, and she became frustrated. Later on, when she found out that Judah is about to join his sheepshearers in Timna, she covered herself with a veil, pretending she is a harlot, and waited for Judah to approach her at the crossroads. As Judah did not recognize her, he was intimate with her. Since he did not have any valuable to pay her, he gave her his seal, cord, and staff as a pledge. She then put on her widow's garb and returned to her father's home. (She reciprocated Judah's behavior with the same "coin" he had paid her—deceit.)

Later on, when Judah sent his friend, the Adumallite, to redeem his pledge for a kid, his friend failed to find her. Judah decided not to further proceed with his inquiry. After three months, he was told that Tamar had played the harlot and was with child by harlotry.

Judah's furious response was that he wished to burn her. At that point, she said that the father of her future

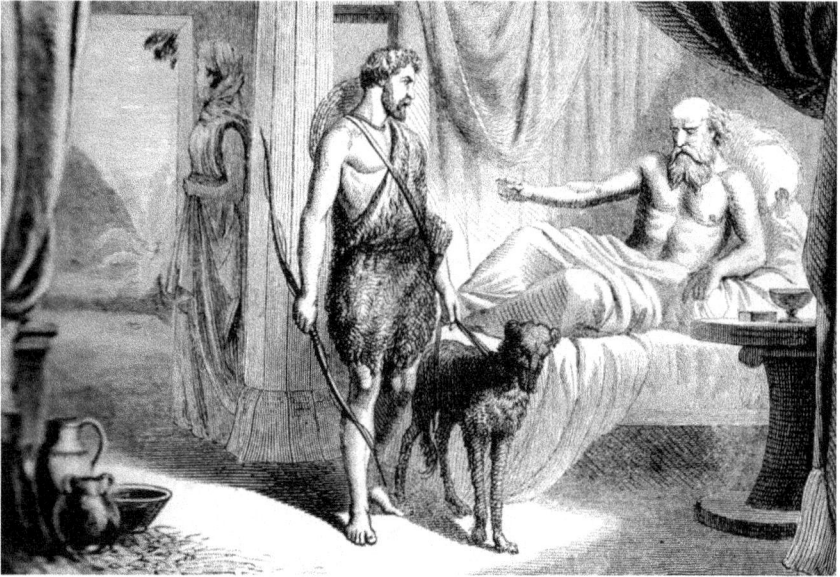

child was the owner of the seal, cord, and staff. Judah recognized them, said she is more just than him, and was not intimate with her anymore.

Eventually, Tamar's story had a happy ending: she gives birth to twin boys, Perez (meaning "to break through") and Zerach (meaning "glowing"). Perez was one of the ancestors of King David, ten generations before David's birth. Indeed, the meaning of Perez is symbolic in this context; his energetic proclivity blazes his trail to future royalty.

Once the reader reaches the conclusion of Judah's/ Tamar's story, is he/she again in a position of wondering why this unexpected story severs so abruptly the story of Joseph, in a point of extreme tension and anxiety?

Scrutinizing comparatively the two stories unearths a ramified, intricate network of analogies between the two accounts. In this respect, the compositional device of severing the continuation of Joseph's story yields a rhetorical device (surprise), since the compositional device affects and directs the way the reader views the story of Joseph. Accordingly, since Tamar's story is a story of hardship that ends happily, and since the story of Joseph is also a story of hardship, does it mean that Joseph's story, like Tamar's, will encounter a happy ending?

The ramified network of compelling analogies between the two stories, the severed one and the severer one, include the following. In Tamar's story, there is leading astray with a piece of clothing— the veil—and absence of recognition on the part of Judah. In Joseph's story, the brothers led Jacob astray with Joseph's ornamented tunic soaked with blood, and Jacob does recognize it.

The recognition motif in both stories was already effectively addressed by Robert Alter in his book, *The Art of Biblical Narrative.* In Joseph's story, Potiphar's wife, who lusts after Joseph, leads astray while Joseph's tunic is in her hand. This way she convinces her husband that Joseph sexually abused her and escaped when she cried and left with her his tunic. In her case and in Judah's, the deceit with a piece of clothing is associated with sexual lust.

Tamar covered herself with a veil (like a harlot), took advantage of Judah's sexual lust, while Potiphar's wife led her husband astray with Joseph's garment after the latter did not respond to her sexual advances.

When Joseph Meets Tamar

While Joseph recognizes his brothers in Egypt, they fail to recognize him (although Joseph recognizes them). In Judah and Tamar's story, Judah fails to recognize Tamar when she covers her face with the veil, pretending to be a harlot.

In Tamar's story, Judah displays much concern about his youngest son, Shelah, and in Joseph's story, Jacob displays the same concern for his youngest son, Benjamin, while refusing to let him join the other brothers in Egypt. In Tamar's story, Judah gives a pledge to Tamar, who pretends to be a harlot, and in Joseph's story, Simon stays at Joseph's as a pledge until Benjamin joins the other brothers in Egypt.

In Joseph's story, young Joseph spies after his brothers and brings to their father bad reports of them (thus acting like a spy) and later, in Egypt, Joseph accuses the brothers for acting as spies. In Tamar's story, there are sinful older brothers (Er and Onan) and in Joseph's story, the elder brothers are equally sinful.

In Tamar's story, Judah promises Tamar (while she pretends to be a harlot) to send her a kid from his flock and in Joseph's story, the deceitful brothers slaughter a kid and dip Joseph's ornamented tunic in the blood, then present it to Jacob, who recognizes it.

As previously noted, in both stories, leading astray with a piece of clothing (Tamar's veil, Joseph's garment), is in the context of sexual lust (Potiphar's wife, Judah).

The analogies between Tamar's and Judah's story introduce the following anxious gap of information: will the analogies between the two stories be completed and

Joseph's story's end will be like in Tamar's story, a happy end? The latter proves to be the case.

Accordingly, Joseph, who meets greatness in Egypt, makes himself known to the brothers and the entire family (including Jacob, the old father and Benjamin, the youngest son) unites in Egypt and enjoys the best of that nation. Therefore, what was initially considered a compositional remiss—inserting Tamar's story in a way that severs Joseph's story at its most acute point of tension and anxiety—is found to be a remarkably sophisticated aesthetic mechanism that combines both composition and rhetoric.

One last comment, partially addressed previously. In Jewish Rabbinical writings, Joseph is depicted as the utmost righteous who refrains from holding grudge to his brothers who abused him so heartlessly. The fact of the matter is the very opposite. Joseph takes revenge at the brothers by intimidating them, by making them dismayed about to their lives, by humiliating them (they keep bowing down to his feet, as anticipated in Joseph's dreams).

Indeed, when Joseph makes himself known to the brothers and hugs and kisses them, they remain motionless (unlike Benjamin), they cannot easily forget how he psychologically tormented them. They are still petrified by their fear of his revenge. That and more. It is found out that the journey between Egypt and Canaan (where Jacob and the brothers resided) was easily doable. Nevertheless, in many years of being in a highest position of power and influence, it did not occur to Joseph to pay a visit to his old, loving father, who mourns him. Indeed, Joseph names his first-born son Menasheh, which derives from the

Hebrew root *n.sh.h.* and means "to forget." Joseph himself provides with the etymological meaning of this word: "God made me forget all my hardship and my father's house." This way, he shamefully fails to remember or to look after his loving, bereft, lamenting father.

That failure to recall ignites a paramount awareness. That awareness reminds the reader that Joseph is not a saint, but rather a "round character" who consists of contradictory characterizations. For instance, Joseph's haughtiness is more than clear: consider his arrogant dreams or his request from his brothers to tell Jacob how elevated his position is in Egypt. However, Joseph is bright, can decipher enigmatic dreams, can predict the future, and is a skillful organizer who cleverly prepares Egypt for pending tribulations of oppressive famine. This way, Joseph is introduced as a flesh-and-blood character, a human character, one who enables the reader to identify wholeheartedly with him.

SOME COMMENTS
OF CONCLUSION

There is an anecdote I find very relevant to a concluding comment, or comments. Here is the anecdote. In an archeological excavation, one of the unearthed relics attracted and kindled considerable curiosity. It was a piece of clay on which text, in an unknown language, was engraved. Archeologists argued with much certainty that it was the most ancient writing that had ever been excavated in the entire world.

It took a very long time to decipher the ancient language in which the writing was composed. Eventually, though, the archeologists met success and they decoded the writing on that piece of clay in the most ancient language ever known. The words on the ancient clay relic read as follows: "What shall I write that has not already been written before?"

Concluding comments feel the same. Whatever I had in mind to write, I already wrote in this book's chapters, as well as in a previous book of mine that also addresses the literariness of the biblical text and the way it serves the text's latent message, *Who Wrought the Bible? Unveiling the Bible's Aesthetic Secrets* (University of Wisconsin Press, 2009).

Both books focus on one scholarly topic: the aesthetic devices, patterns, and mechanisms of the biblical text and

the way in which they are used to convey and enhance the biblical text's latent ideological message (liturgical, ideological, moral, legal, social, historical, educational, and pedagogical). Indeed, in each and every biblical text that carries a certain message, the nature of the "enlisted" and activated aesthetic device, pattern, and mechanism may change accordingly. Nevertheless, in many cases the aesthetic device, pattern, and mechanism are quite the same, such as a compositional device that consists of the way the text is organized, or constructed; or a rhetorical device that consists of surprise (while using the dynamic quality of the textual sequence) that is embodied by frustrated expectations.

In many cases, both compositional and rhetorical devices are causally connected: the rhetorical device stems from the compositional device and both of them, simultaneously, turn into an aesthetic mechanism that effectively serves a certain bulk of biblical text.

That and more. This book focuses on some of the most, intriguing characters in the Hebrew Bible: Adam, Eve, Terrah, Abraham, Moses, Isaac, Esau, Ishmael, Hagar, Joseph, Naomi, Joseph's brothers, Sarah, Samson, Ruth, Jonah, David, psalmist Esther, Noah, the Israelites in the Sinai desert, Joshua, the spies, the sons of Noah (Shem, Ham, and Japheth), the builders of the Tower of Babel, Tamar.

Indeed, each of the characters is considerably different from one another. However, very similar aesthetic devices, patterns, and mechanisms are inlaid in presenting those characters' chronicles, unveiling different characteristics in each and every character. In all cases, applying a careful, close reading to those biblical texts provides with exciting findings that had been concealed so far.

That and more. Applying the tools of literary investigation to the biblical text acts in the capacity of efficient means that enable the reader to learn about the Bible's artistic intricacy and the way it serves the latent ideological messages of the biblical text. Indeed, following this vein, this book (as well as the previous one), by using those literary techniques of investigation, cast new, surprising light on some of the most prominent, equally tantalizing characters and chronicles in the Bible.

For instance, righteous Noah is found to be less righteous than commonly believed. Samson is found to be the worst leader ever of the Israelites as well as pitifully childish. Joseph is revealed as being cruel and vindictive. Young David is found to be greedy and arrogant and even God Himself is found to lack self-confidence in the story of the Tower of Babel.

Nevertheless, the shortcomings of those biblical characters do not necessarily belittle their merits. Those shortcomings make those biblical characters more human, characters who can be judged compassionately. In this respect, the biblical-literary studies amalgamated in this book make the reader understand better not only the artistic intricacy of the biblical text, but also the human aspects of its characters.

ACKNOWLEDGMENTS

I am obliged to my good friend, Raphael (Raphi) Kadushin, senior editor at the University of Wisconsin Press, for giving me permission to use some material from a previous book of mine, *Who Wrought the Bible? Unveiling the Bible's Aesthetic Secrets* (UW Press, 2009).

I am equally obliged to my good friend and publisher, Kira Henschel, for her ongoing support, generosity, limitless patience, unconditional friendship, and praiseworthy professional work.

ABOUT THE AUTHOR

Dr. Yair Mazor is a professor of modern Hebrew literature and biblical literature with the University of Wisconsin–Milwaukee. Professor Mazor is the author of 28 books and over 250 articles and critical reviews. Dr. Mazor's fields of study are modern Hebrew literature, Enlightenment Hebrew literature in the 19th centuries in Eastern Europe, biblical literature, comparative literature, Scandinavian literature, and Hebrew children's literature.

Dr. Mazor has earned numerous scholarly awards, among them the Shpam Prize and Dov Sadan Prize from the University of Tel Aviv for two of his books; the Baron Prize for exceptional excellence in research in the field of Jewish Studies; the "Distinguished Undergraduate Teaching Award" from the University of Wisconsin–Milwaukee; and a national award, the "Most Distinguished Scholar of Hebrew Studies in the USA, the Friedman Prize.

In his military service, Dr. Mazor acted as a combat paratrooper, as well as an instructor of parachuting.

www.ingramcontent.com/pod-product-compliance
Lightning Source LLC
Chambersburg PA
CBHW070350090426
42733CB00009B/1356